Painter's Workshop

An exploration of the studio

Painter's Workshop
an exploration of the studio

Catherine Moody

B T BATSFORD LTD   LONDON

For my father Victor Hume Moody over whose studio the branches of the tree of tradition live, grow and bear fruit.

© Catherine Moody 1982
First published 1982

All rights reserved. No part of this publication may be reproduced, in any form or by any means, without permission from the Publisher
ISBN 0 7134 1317 4

Filmset in Monophoto Univers by
Latimer Trend & Company Ltd, Plymouth

Printed and bound
in Great Britain by
The Pitman Press Ltd
Bath

for the publishers
B T Batsford Ltd
4 Fitzhardinge Street
London W1H 0AH

CONTENTS

Acknowledgment

The author wishes to thank the following:

Miss Harriet Dyer Adams for help in obtaining reproductions from USA.

Birmingham Museums and Art Gallery for the colour plate of *The Hat Shop* by Henry Tonks.

Ms Irene Briers for permission to adapt text and use illustrations from 'Painter's Workshop' articles in *Leisure Painter*.

R T Cowern RA for figure 18 *the Pigeon Loft* and research for chapter 16.

Michael Dinkel RWS, ARCA, RWA for research in chapters 10 and 11.

Bernard Dunstan RA for demonstration painting figure 88 *Two Nudes and the Flowered Screen 1979*.

The Museum of Fine Arts, Boston, Massachusetts for permission to reproduce figure 64, *The Artist in his Studio* by Rembrandt, from the Zoe Oliver Sherman collection, given in memory of Lillie Oliver Poor.

Gareth Hawker RA, Sch Cert MA Fine Art for research in chapter 15.

Norman Hepple RA for research and figures 77 and 78.

The Estate of Robert Frost for permission to use the quotation on page 9 from *Collected Poems by Robert Frost* published by Jonathan Cape Limited.

John McLellan for research in chapter 18.

Victor Hume Moody for figures 27, 53, 54, 55, 56, 58, 59 and 65.

The Trustees of the National Gallery, London for figure 15 *The Marriage of Giovanni Arnolfini and Giovanna Cernami*.

Peter Owen Limited for permission to use the quotation on page 7 from the writings of Jean Cocteau.

Miss Constance-Anne Parker, Librarian, The Royal Academy, Burlington House, London, for data from RA Schools archives.

Mrs Lynda Rogac for the silver point flower study figure 57.

Sir John Rothenstein CBE, KC St G, former director of the Tate Gallery, London with Michael Rothenstein for the colour plate of *The Doll's House* by Sir William Rothenstein.

Sir John Rothenstein and Michael Rothenstein ATA with the Graves Art Gallery, City Art Galleries, Sheffield for figure 24 *Self Portrait* by Sir William Rothenstein, and for figure 35 *Eli the Thatcher* by Sir William Rothenstein with the City Art Gallery, Manchester.

The Royal Borough of Kensington and Chelsea Libraries and Arts Service for Lord Leighton's Studio figure 85.

The Rt Hon Mr Speaker, The House of Commons for figures 26(a) and 26(b) *Sir Thomas Roe at the Mōghul Court 1614* by Sir William Rothenstein.

William Sly Mal Dip, for copy of LeGros portrait, figure 23.

The Tate Gallery, London for figure 16 George Moore by Walter Richard Sickert, and colour plate of *The Doll's House* by Sir William Rothenstein.

Mrs M Theodas for information for figures 79, 80 and 81.

John Ward RA for his original drawing The Studio, Bilting, figure 72.

All other line drawings, diagrams and paintings, unless otherwise stated, are by the author, Catherine Moody.

Introduction

The more a poet sings in his genealogical tree, the more his singing is in tune. Jean Cocteau

To explain the title of this book, I might say that it is an exploration of the studio in company with some masters of painting, some apprentices, some teachers and some students, and with all those who are curious to know more. To tell a little about my own exploration is the least I can do for those who may be considering accompanying me.

A painter, designer and craftswoman, I was a student under my father Victor Hume Moody who was Principal of Malvern School of Art. Indeed I was his pupil from my earliest school days when he initiated me in the mystery of drawing in perspective a two-inch cube, standing on the ground at an angle to the picture plane, with the use of vanishing points, measuring points and a distance point – a very useful piece of knowledge to have already absorbed when greater complexities were to be added. Furthermore, his constant example has shown me the intensity and depth of research possible in pursuing a true visual interpretation.

Student also of the Royal College of Art, and the Birmingham School of Art, I learned yet more from John Holmes, Principal of Manchester School of Art where I first taught.

In Malvern I took up where my father left off becoming Head of Department of the School of Art, then associated with the Malvern College of Further Education.

To save confusion caused by the many changes of title of the School of Art, I retain the title of Malvern School of Art throughout this book. Founded in 1887 the School's official name has varied and there may yet be further changes, but except for the title the School has been kept 'on course' and its direction has been set on scholarship and good craftsmanship in fine art and craft.

As a student, teacher and administrator and as a practising artist I have found there was always much to learn from all those I encountered who were dedicated to the work in hand. I cannot name everybody, many were unconscious that they had added to my store, but I should like to thank very much R T Cowern RA, Dean of the Faculty of Art and Design and Associate Director, Brighton Polytechnic for his numerous visits to Malvern, to share with my students and me, the fruits of his wide scholarship and deep understanding of art. During the writing of this book research has been made a delightful pursuit by his enthusiastic participation and help on many points. Bernard Dunstan RA too has been very generous in giving us the fruits of his experience.

Diana Armfield, at the same time and Norman Hepple RA, most recently, have joined in this generous pooling of the findings of those who know the workings of the studio.

When the ideals of a representational painter were most bitterly rejected, I derived great encouragement from John Ward RA, who so good humouredly brandished the flag at the conference table, for a level-headed approach to the problems of painting and then showed us how he practised what he stood for in two demonstration paintings.

From the little boy who explained there were 'H' pencils that were hard and 'B' pencils that were soft and black; with the many teachers I have seen in action; to Georges Aczel, the expert on the construction of Old Master Paintings; to Gilbert Spencer RA and B Fleetwood-Walker RA a most enlivening teacher; to Dame Laura Knight, a great encourager; to Sir John Rothenstein CBE, KCStG for kindly reading and augmenting my chapter on Sir William Rothenstein's work; to Mr Percy Grieve QC, MP for Solihull for bringing current news of the condition of the Rothenstein mural in St Stephen's Hall and to Major Victor le Fanu, Assistant Serjeant at Arms of the House of Commons for making a reproduction of the mural available; to Miss Constance-Anne Parker, Librarian of the

Royal Academy for research on more than one subject; to David Alston, Deputy Curator, Christ Church Picture Gallery, Oxford and to the staff of several picture galleries and libraries here and in the USA, not least of Malvern Public Library, whose interest and help have been most valuable; to the students who have joined with me in hunting up Cennini's recipes and who have co-operated in trying out materials in more extensive tests than I could have done on my own; to all those who, in the studios I have worked in, have added to the store of knowledge that I have been able to make available in the visit to the Painter's Workshop, I am most grateful. Of all pursuits it is the one that brings most friends and most delight on the journey of exploration.

Although I have spent my time in the painter's workshop, it was not until Ms Irene Briers, Editorial Director of the periodical *Leisure Painter* made the suggestion that I should contribute occasional articles under this title that I realised that here was a way that I could answer many questions that I had been asked and had been able to answer, up to now, only in the ephemeral form of teaching, lecturing and demonstrating. 'Cherry' Briers' constant encouragement has meant that a considerable amount of material accumulated and again through her suggestion I have envisaged it in book form. The apostrophe has moved back one letter from the Painters' of *Leisure Painter* to my own Painter's Workshop.

The far seeing and careful guidance of Thelma M Nye, Senior Editor of Batsford has brought it to a point where it emerges between hard covers. Here I have been enabled to go farther afield for appropriate examples and there is more scope for illustration. The book has also received from master painters now at work, contributions from their studios which brings us right up to the vanguard of artistic activity.

Wise words in season from the author, Geoffrey Trease, some dotting of the 'i's' from Malvern Writers' Circle, some practical help from W A Hayens, Principal, Malvern Hills College, and much care in typing by Mrs Marion Hughes have all enabled me to produce this book.

For those who may like to look something up whilst setting out their palettes, or for those who, having enjoyed pictures either by making them or by looking at them, may like to browse, I hope that this account of our journeyings may engender a feeling of fellowship throughout the whole tradition of painting.

'Men work together,' I told him from the heart,
'Whether they work together or apart.'

Robert Frost

1 The painter in oils

The palette

If you ride your bicycle successfully you do not pause to think out how to adjust your balance before swerving to avoid a brick in the road.

When you paint, a message travels from your subject through your eye to the brain and from the brain through your arm and brush point to the canvas. This message should be as uninterrupted as that from the brick when you are riding the bicycle. If the message to the handle-bars falters, you fall. If the message to the tip of the brush falters, your brush stroke loses balance and your picture falls, if not to the ground, at least some way short of its impelled and inspired statement.

How much better it is if your paint, palette, brush and medium all work together so that the paint is carried to the chosen point in a telling, expressive stroke.

The foul and messy palette crusted with old paint, the bunch of grotty brushes – sometimes the affectation of the genius who seeks to suggest that his soul is above such material things – is not much help to the student and in any case not all geniuses are messy workers – far from it.

The first essential in a palette is that it should balance on the thumb. It is the least tiring to hold and is easy to keep level. A kidney shaped palette is the best for this. It should be sandpapered quite thin underneath, on the outer side (A–A–A in sketch) and be quite thick and heavy on the part nearer the body (B–B–B in sketch). The kidney shape is the handiest in movement and keeps all your pigments within easy radius. Make sure that you use it the right way up and then the chamfer on the hole will fit round the thumb.

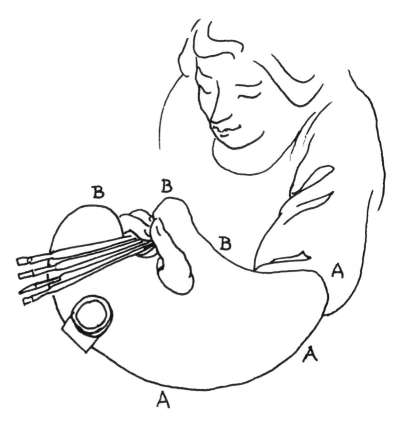

If you carry your paints about then you may need a square palette to fit in the box. Even this can be improved by sandpapering the outside corner underneath to make it balance better. However it can never equal the kidney shape for being ideally suited to the action of painting.

Other palettes may come in handy for special purposes. I often use a rectangular palette only 10 in. – 25 cm long, but I use this because it is light and has a lovely surface for mixing and, being so small, it encourages me to clean up and re-mix, which sometimes is a good thing.

As soon as you get a new palette, coat it on both sides with linseed oil. Leave if for half an hour, then rub it over with another coat and polish it off after a further half hour interval. Every time you finish painting, clean off *all* the paint and polish the palette with a clean cotton rag. Very soon you will have a fine surface, very pleasant as a ground for mixing the paint in the colour, tone and consistency that you need. If you have paint over, never leave it on the palette 'for the next time'. Scrape off each colour with a palette knife and put it in a fold of polythene. There is nothing that interrupts the flow of thought more effectively than to attempt to mix the required colour with pigment that turns out to be dry. By the time that you have discovered that *nothing* is coming off the hard knob of paint, your vision of what you wanted to express fades and dies. Nothing leads you 'up a gum tree' so much as old dry paint. A well-ordered palette on the other hand, is the most helpful means to your objective.

Note   A palette specially cut in reverse for left handed painters is obtainable but you will have to search for it.

2 Oil painting

The palette – the order of colours

When you have your well balanced and well polished palette resting comfortably on your arm, what is the next step?

It is a good idea to establish a certain order in which to place your colours. Then you can move your brush in approximately the right direction without having to look. Indeed you may have your eye resting on your subject whilst your brush is on its way for more supplies of white or whatever is wanted, and a quick glance will suffice to secure what you need. Avoid, at all costs, the long search.

It is best to put your squeezes of pigment round the outside of your palette, so that you can bring a dab from each squeeze nearer to you to do the mixing in the space under your eye, and it does not much matter what order you use for your pigments on the palette so long as you establish *one* order and stick to it.

My own arrangement, based on a kind of time and motion study, is to have the white, which one needs to mix with nearly everything, in a central position. To the left of the white I put the cool and the dark colours: black, blue and green. To the right I put the warm colours: the reds and yellows. Thus I can move the brush in the direction of warm colours before I decide whether it is orange, vermilion or cadmium orange that I need. Moving over to the left for something cool I can start mixing in some terra vert and then secure a little viridian if required.

Going through the portfolio of William Etty's drawings in the Library of the Victoria and Albert Museum, I found that Etty had made a chart of Richard Wilson's palette. At first it appeared that there were about 45 colours on the palette, which seemed a rather

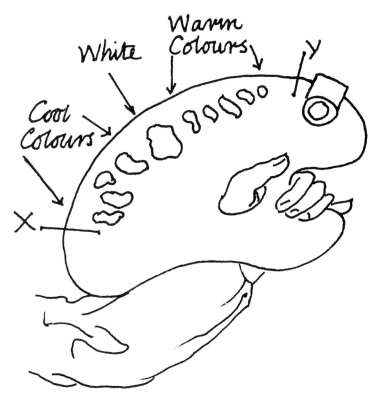

Everything beyond X gets on your sleeve. Leave a space beyond Y for your dipper

A – light red; B – yellow ochre; C – flake white; D – ivory black. Mixed colour patch 1 = A and C mixed to produce a rosy pink; 2 = B and C mixed producing primrose; 3 = D and C mixed producing dove grey tending to blue

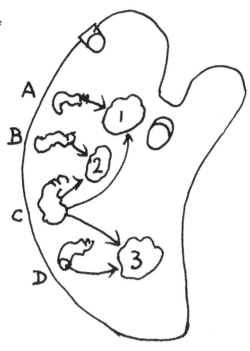

Yellow ochre, white and black mixed producing 4 – a useful greenish grey. Light red, white and black are another useful trio giving a purplish grey. These mixtures with white show the potentialities of the two earth colours and black and reveal what richness of colour these simple means will produce

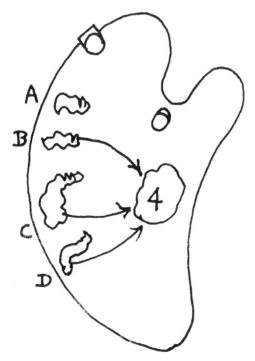

liberal allowance but on reading the notes I found that there was a fairly moderate selection of pigments put out initially and all the pairs of pigments were mixed and then the trios and so on through a great number of permutations.

I find it useful to mix on my palette firstly light red and white and see the pleasant rosy colour this makes; then white and yellow ochre, then white and ivory black making a useful blue grey. Then I mix a trio – ivory black, white and yellow ochre which produces a grey that is markedly greenish. It is worth doing this whilst palette and brushes are clean. Later, when you have been mixing everything together it is difficult to get these pure tints that simple mixtures give. Perhaps this is what Richard Wilson was doing and what interested Etty in recording it.

When you put your paints out leave a space at the right hand for your dipper. A metal dipper with a sprung flange or clip on the bottom is what you need. This means that your medium is on the route to the mixing place. You can pick up the medium on the brush on the way to the paint without hesitation. This is much better than the old jam jar on a table or window sill. See that the spring of the clip holds tight and then you can move about carrying your medium wherever you go and you won't knock it over when you lean forward to land a vital stroke.

3 Something in the dipper or turps

All artists pray for inspiration; its coming is partly beyond control.

It is difficult to paint a masterpiece and so it is as well to remove all impediments before a start is made. An inspired work can be frustrated before it is begun.

Artists' quality paint is the best and on the whole most economical to use being more brilliant and more pure than student quality.

When it comes to the choice of a medium, there is a temptation to go to the back of the garage to find something to put in the dipper from the selection of odds and ends left over from house painting. The urge should be resisted. As much care should be exercised over the choice of the medium as over the paint.

Oil paints are ground in linseed oil (or in poppy oil which yellows less). The tube pigment is usually ground in a fairly generous amount of oil and often this is sufficient medium for painting purposes. Extra oil in the dipper is not usually needed.

Turpentine is the most favoured all-purpose medium. It dilutes the paint and enables the canvas to be covered quickly, especially in the initial 'lay in' or monochrome stage. It evaporates so that in about three minutes the very fluid paint is established firmly on the canvas.

Generally spoken of as 'turps', various things can appear in the dipper under this general term. A good deal has been written about white spirit, a refined petroleum spirit. It evaporates quickly, leaves no stain, is colourless and is comparatively cheaper than turpentine.

For my own work I would always use best quality English distilled turpentine because it dissolves the paint more completely. It is a highly refined essential oil derived from fir and

The urge to find the odd bottle from the back of the garage, left over from the house painting, must be resisted

13

Drapery with Jug and Bowl 10 in. × 12½ in. (25 cm × 31 cm). A painting done with turps alone; a raw umber monochrome laid in with the paint thin and wet, scrubbed in at speed, allowing the paint to trickle down and then catching it with the brush, working with freedom and plenty of fluid paint. The turps evaporated in a few minutes leaving the paint surface in good condition for further painting in the next stage

pine tree resin. It is colourless and should be stored in the dark. White spirit mixes with, but turpentine unites more completely with the oil in the paint.

As it dissolves the pigment, as it flows from the brush, I find its handling quality superior to that of white spirit.

Once whilst watching John Ward RA paint, I heard one of the students ask, 'What constitutes *bad paint quality*?' John Ward replied 'It is when the paint goes like cold Irish stew on the palette.' For me, white spirit encourages this sort of thing.

Some students complain of the expense of the best turpentine but this need not be a burden if it is kept strictly for its proper use. More than a dessert spoonful should never be put in the dipper at one time. Then little is lost if the dipper is tilted and some is spilt. Furthermore it is much better to use turps freshly from the bottle. It should not be allowed to air off; it should be used up and then a little more put out. Nor is it a good thing to keep a large bottle three parts empty. It is worth decanting into a small bottle with an airtight cap, the object being to keep the turps without air in the bottle.

Some people keep a jar of turps to rinse their brushes in, but this seems to me to confuse oil painting with watercolour painting when the brush is constantly washed out in water. If the brush gets too full and dirty with oil paint it should be pinched in a fold of newspaper squeezing from the ferrule to the tip and again with the paint rag. Then the brush will be clean enough, properly shaped and it will not be soggy and wet as it is if rinsed in turps. It will be ready to take up paint at the right consistency.

Cheap genuine turpentine from the ironmonger is good for a brush cleaner and is the only thing to clean resin medium or varnish from brush, hands, palette or dipper but it is not good enough to paint with. It can go dark and leave a brown sticky deposit. After cleaning brushes in ironmonger's turps, it is a good plan to dry them on a rag and then give a final rinse in best turps. Often there is enough left in the dipper to do this. When the work is finished the paint rag should be pushed in and wiped round the dipper so that it is clean and polished for the next day.

'Paint fat over lean' is an old maxim and a good one. It means that a painting should be started without any oil, thinned only with turps. Then, each day the painting continues, a little more medium can be used. Finally, paint heavily charged with oil or resin medium, can come into play. If paint is used that is thinned with turps in the later stages, when heavy paintwork has been used initially, the turps-laden brushstrokes will sink in, go dead, and fail to 'tell' as part of the painting. Furthermore a 'fat' medium in the first layers is prevented, by subsequent layers, from drying out properly and the stresses and strains of shrinkage in drying tend to encourage cracking. A 'lean' layer in the early stages dries out as the painting progresses. When painting the initial monochrome diluted with turps, using it thin and wet, the paint can be allowed to trickle down, be scrubbed over a large area at speed so that it runs together of its own accord, draw with in line, or blocked in with thin pigment. All this can be done with the turps evaporating in a few minutes and the paint quality will remain lively and good. This is one of the best foundations for the next stage and for complex further development.

Turpentine must be kept clean. A dirty brush must never be put in the bottle. The bottle must be kept in a dark place, and the cap must always be screwed on tightly.

4 The paint rag

This chapter is on the humblest and the least considered of the painter's aids - the paint rag. It is however a most important item without which the painter will be at a loss.

It can be used not only for cleaning up, but also to draw on a dark wet canvas, wiping out the lights. This can be a correction or a deliberate method of developing the drawing.

Newspapers, tissues, or a kitchen roll are all helpful but do not take the place of a large piece of cotton cloth – usually a cotton sheet, retired from its place on the bed when a split appears. It is usually handy to have one clean paint rag and one which has already done some service and can be used to wipe off a palette knife if you are removing some offending colour or tone. If the knife is not wiped clean *each time*, it will return the unwanted paint to the canvas in a new place.

Dame Laura Knight once said to me, 'You want a *lot* of *clean* paint rags. I always have a great many.' Then, after reflecting, she continued 'I once saved a man's life through having a clean paint rag.' She went on to tell me how she had been painting in a circus – a subject she made very much her own. She told how one morning the lion trainer was made to do the act for the press photographers. He was asked to repeat the act again and again so that the press could get the shots they wanted. This was seriously interrupting the normal rhythm of the usual morning rehearsal of the lions' act and the animals became restless and bored. One lion made a wide sweep with his paw – not intending to make an attack – but he caught the trainer across the forehead with his claws before turning away. The claws drew blood – the trainer was half blinded with it running into his eyes. He covered what he could with his hand lest the lion scenting blood would have been excited to attack. Dame Laura, seeing it all from her sketching stool just outside the cage, thrust her large clean paint rag through the bars to the trainer, who, engulfing his gory forehead in its folds, was able to back cautiously towards the exit and get out before the animals were aware that anything was amiss.

Not every painter will have such exciting episodes with paint rags. But a palette can be given a really good polish with rags when cleaning up so that when it is next taken down for use it gleams in a really encouraging way and is an invitation to the mixing of the paint.

As well as a rag it is necessary to have plenty of newspaper, preferably cut up into pieces before work commences. Tissues or a kitchen roll can be used but cost more. Although a kitchen roll has perforations so that pieces can be pulled off, it is very difficult to get a piece off with one hand. I have found kitchen rolls bouncing around on the studio floor or students trying to hold a roll down with a foot when trying to get a piece off without relinquishing the palette. Again it is best to get a pile of separate sheets before starting to paint.

Dame Laura Knight told me how she came to the lion trainer's rescue with a clean paint rag. This was whilst she was making studies for one of her paintings of the circus and circus people

5 Cold pressed linseed oil

In Chapter 3, I discussed the use of English distilled turpentine. I placed it first as the most useful liquid to have in the dipper. It also comes first in the early stages of painting.

I will describe a number of traditional media, many unfamiliar to the student today. This should enable you to explore the field and thereby make your own choice. There are certain practical factors to be weighed up in the choice of a painting vehicle, and there is also the aspect of your own temperament. The way you handle your paint is part of your nature and you should endeavour to find that which is most in accord with your kind of handling.

A student taking up oil painting for the first time often leaves the artists' suppliers with a large bottle of linseed oil. He or she is going to do Oil Painting so here is The Oil!

No – the linseed oil of oil painting is in the tube. Ground in linseed (or poppy oil) the pigment is brought to the right consistency for paint. In the dipper, unlimited oil is undesirable. The blends of oil, with diluents and with resins is the field that needs investigating.

Up to the end of the nineteenth century any painting executed with a reasonable degree of skill displayed a variety of paint surface that was extremely sympathetic to the subject matter. There are numerous recipes evolved by various artists. None of these mixtures can produce a great painting of its own accord – but, if a painter's conception is to be conveyed with full force and effectiveness, he must needs find the painting vehicle that gives him an untrammelled range of expression. For instance, without the right medium a full range of tone cannot be encompassed.

To enable the student to explore this field it is a good idea to be able to find one's way about the three main categories involved:

1 The diluents or solvents sometimes known as 'essential' or 'ethereal' oils

   a English distilled turpentine

   b Oil of spike, a beautifully perfumed diluent which is prepared from lavender

   c White spirit – refined petroleum solvent.

All these evaporate quickly. Paint mixed with them to a free flowing – even trickling – consistency is firm on the canvas in about 10 to 15 minutes.

2 The drying oils

   a Linseed oil

   b Poppy oil

These oils dry of their own accord. They are the body which holds the dry ground pigment together. They can be naturally or chemically processed. Natural processing is by far the preferable.

3 Resins which form varnishes and painting vehicles

   a Dammar resin

   b Fossil copal resin

   c Mastic resin

   d Gum arabic

   e Venice turpentine.

These resins come from many parts of the world.

Now to investigate linseed oil. First of all it is necessary to obtain cold pressed linseed oil (CPLO). This is the naturally processed oil produced by Winsor and Newton. It is far superior to ordinary refined linseed oil. The painter Gluck did a great deal of research – even detective work – in the 1960s to isolate this product. The point about cold pressed linseed oil is that only as much oil is expressed from the seeds (common cultivated flax, *Linum usitatissimum*) as will drain out without heat. If any heat is applied to the seed in the presses more oil will come out *but* it contains undesirable extras such as proteins, acids and fats. Cold pressed linseed oil is clear, has good handling qualities, is a good dryer and does not shine or glint whilst you are painting.

Gluck, a painter of distinction and an authority on painters' methods and materials, did much good research in the field of the permanence of artists' materials. Two of her papers are noted in the bibliography. The two lectures she gave at Malvern School of Art in June 1965, and the ensuing discussion and subsequent letters were full of vital information.

Gluck had run CPLO to earth a little time before her visit and we had begun to use it in preference to refined linseed oil. I was able to discuss with her the value of this discovery – the most evident being its good handling qualities, and its freedom from the glint or 'suede effect'. This is an impediment to working on and overpainting when work has gone on for some days on one canvas. We have since used CPLO for the preparation of sun thickened oil, with excellent results.

All linseed oil tends to darken in time. A painting that has been in a clean atmosphere but in a dark cupboard will go dark. If you put the painting out in the not too hot sun for an hour or two it will come back to its original tone. If you cover a part with a piece of thick card you can see how much lighter the exposed part becomes.

Oils to be avoided are:

1   Oils containing dryers which darken the oil a great deal

2   Boiled oil from the builders' merchants

3   Cheap linseed oil which may be adulterated with non-drying oil and has the effect of making a painting look as if it has been wrapping fish and chips. I have had this sad experience of getting oil on cartridge paper that evidently had been 'cut' with whale oil and it *never* dried!

The virtues of cold pressed linseed oil known as CPLO

Sunlight has a reviving effect on linseed oil that has darkened. A card clamped over one corner of a canvas will, in a few hours, show how much it can change. That part in the sun will become less yellow or obscure and colour will become more true

6 Sun Thickened Linseed Oil

In the exploration of the various vehicles and media, linseed can first be tried in the two states to which it can be changed from the raw condition, namely sun thickened oil and stand oil. These have been used probably since the beginning of the oil painting.

In a district where the air is clean and free from petrol fumes it is worth while making sun thickened linseed oil in the garden or on a balcony. It can be purchased but there is something to be said for making your own. A batch we made in 1977 is now of a pale colour like a light white wine. A bottle of commercially made sun thickened or fat oil purchased a little before this is now quite an orange beery colour.

Sun thickened cold pressed linseed oil in the sun and fresh air. A summer in the garden turns CPLO into a very useful painting vehicle – a valuable ingredient of a blended medium

When you make your own, it is best to use cold pressed linseed oil – obtainable from Winsor and Newton. Half fill a number of clean one pound honey jars with the CPLO. Protect from suicidal midges and flies by covering with muslin or thin nylon stocking tied on with string. Expose these jars to the light and air whenever the weather is fine. Keep them on a tray which you bring in at night. Shake and move the jars gently every day to prevent a skin forming. At the end of a good summer it will become a beautiful blond thick oil which remains pale and is reluctant to darken.

In the sample illustrated I have painted some strokes with a brush loaded with flake white with sun thickened oil on a darkened ground to show what characteristics this oil displays. I put about a teaspoonful of the sun thickened oil in the dipper and used it to mix with some flake white on the palette with a hog brush. Thick and honey-like it does not flow far. It holds a generous brushload of pigment and laying it on a heavily toothed canvas it holds its rounded oily shape and ends up with a scumble of thick paint on the high points of the canvas weave. It does not soak into the canvas and thereby enables the underpainting to sparkle through. In the sample the strokes with sun thickened oil lie to the left. Next I put two drops of crystal dammar varnish (produced by Robersons, Parkway, London) into the oil in the dipper. With this I did the strokes to the right of the sample. The pigment held up even better and facilitated the sort of movement of the brush that could be expressive if need be. Lastly, I added six drops of English distilled turpentine. With this I was able to get a thin but complete cover of pigment such as is

Brush strokes painted with sun thickened cold pressed linseed oil made at home in the garden in 1977. The brush strokes on the left have sun thickened CPLO mixed with flake white. The strokes on the right have the addition of a small amount of crystal dammar varnish. The areas at the bottom of the sample have turps added to facilitate the painting out of a flat area

needed in the early stages of a painting. And so sun thickened oil shows itself to be a useful state in which to use linseed oil, which with the addition of dammar or turpentine has properties of some diversity, allowing the painter an interesting range of activity. Its clear paleness allows your light and delicate pinks or blues to be pure and not tinged with an obtrusive yellow. Used by Rubens and others it allows a great amount of technical freedom and has good lasting qualities.

7 Copal oil medium

Copal oil medium, one of the most delightful of media, a most time honoured aid to the painter of the eighteenth and nineteenth centuries, has been freely available up to the 1950s. It should be yellowish – rather the colour of mild ale.

The only copal available from the leading suppliers that I have been able to find is a black liquid resembling the concoction that used to be put on floors to imitate dark oak. It is therefore useless for painting. A painting medium should be as colourless as possible so that it does not distort the colour of the pigment. The yellow and amber of good copal and good linseed oil are tolerated because of their great qualities in bonding the pigment and producing excellent handling qualities as well as durability.

Probing the marshlands with long spears, the members of the rural communities of various tropical regions used to produce a constant supply of good quality fossil copal resin. They had a skill in finding it, a skill which must have been passed on for generations. When their probes hit a solid lump they fished it up and in this way supplies of excellent fossil copal were made available. To European artists of centuries ago this rare and valuable resin was brought from these remote and little known places. This is evidenced by the paintings of the past whose qualities arise from the use of this most durable of resins. Now, wars and civil strife have disrupted the rural communities of more than one area of the tropical latitudes. The rustic skills seem to be forgotten, and the supply of fossil copal has fairly abruptly withered away.

A painter's only hope at present is to search

Copal oil medium is at present under something of a cloud

for old stock of copal oil medium or copal varnish. Look in the back of your cupboard in the studio to see if you have a bottle left over from the 1950s, treasure it and use it when you intend to paint a masterpiece.

8 Stand oil

Chapter 6 showed how a summer in the garden produced sun thickened oil from cold pressed linseed oil. The other most useful condition of linseed oil is stand oil. Opposite treatments are used to produce these two states. Sun thickened oil is exposed to as much sun and oxygen as possible. Stand oil, on the other hand, is heated in the absence of air (polymerized). Both oils are time honoured in their use. They are durable and protect the pigment, and dry more quickly than untreated oil. Sun thickened oil is very pale and can be almost colourless. Stand oil is thick, unctuous and like golden syrup falls from the bottle in a 'dollop'. It makes its own characteristic brush stroke (see paint samples illustrated here). With turps added it makes a long stroke. It is a 'long' medium in contrast to one which breaks short and is buttery. Stand oil retains its rich oily appearance without much loss in drying.

I recall the old saying 'Paint fat over lean'. *Lean* means paint diluted with turps or any essential oil which spreads the paint a long way and then evaporates entirely. It does not bind or protect the pigment, but it forms a good basis on which to work. The 'fat' medium then used on top is the exposed surface and is able to dry in its own good time. There are then no problems of cracking through conflicting rates of drying. It is characteristic of stand oil that a brush stroke settles into its own rounded form. (See paint samples.) It can be diluted with turps — needing a vigorous stir in the dipper to mix it. To this can be added a very small amount of dammar varnish and the mixture stirred again. Its nature is to settle down into an even solid surface.

It is very much a matter of temperament

C.O.Moody

Artists of the sixteenth and seventeenth centuries valued 'cold drawn' linseed oil (ie CPLO) that had been kept for many years. The term for this seems to have been 'stand oil'. Now the name is applied to linseed oil that is polymerized (ie oil heated in the absence of oxygen)

whether you favour a 'long' or a 'short' medium. Some people like to apply their paint in short mosaic like facets — others like a vehicle which will follow a linear approach to the job in hand. As can be seen in the right hand sample of stand oil it lends itself to a plastic modelling of rounded form.

It is worthwhile giving each painting vehicle a trial to find out what suits you best.

The order of working could most simply be on the following lines. To explore these painting vehicles a trial should be made beginning with the simplest preparation. This sequence can be used:

(A) Pigment straight from the tube

(B) Pigment straight from the tube with turps added.

(C1) Pigment with *sun thickened* CPLO added.

(D1) Pigment with *stand oil* added.

(C2) Add to this an equal measure of turps.

(D2) Add to this an equal measure of turps.

(C3) Add a scrap of dammar varnish or more turps as required.

(D3) Add a scrap of dammar varnish or more turps as required.

Students of Malvern School of Art under a member of staff John McLellan have, over a considerable period, been getting very satisfactory results using stand oil with turps and sometimes a little dammar varnish. Stand oil varies with each supplier. Some can be very unsatisfactory and some I have seen used, caused the paint to slip down the canvas hours after the painting session, but Winsor and Newton supply a reliable product.

In further discussion with the painter and researcher Gluck I learned more about the traditional stand oil as well as the cold pressing of the raw linseed. The term stand oil, Gluck suggested, was difficult to translate from German or Flemish writings with any accuracy and it may have meant simply oil that has stood corked up for a long time. If a bottle is quite full there is little room for air, and oxidation could be minimal. This point distinguishes stand oil from sun thickened oil which has the maximum exposure to oxidation. It is also differentiated from today's polymerized oil in that it may not have been heated.

Stand oil has been used chiefly in Northern Europe and the two states of linseed oil, stand and sun thickened, have been around for many centuries and both can be used with confidence. The possibility that stand oil may be prepared in either of two ways is a subject worth pursuing but the modern preparation recommended above is well tested.[1]

This initial exploration into painting methods and the many painting vehicles that have been evolved, will be carried further in later chapters but in the meantime an impediment to progress will be investigated. Practical difficulties may be overcome and yet a bar to the next step of development may make itself apparent.

The origins of some inhibitions about the use of painting vehicles that lurk in the background today need to be brought into the light.

Stand oil with flake white. *Left to right*; the stand oil is so stiff that it has to be mixed with the pigment with a palette knife. The strokes put on with a palette knife soon settle into a rounded form. The facets made by the knife are not retained by this vehicle – 1 and 2. Stirred vigorously with turps the hog hair brush carries the paint a little further, but it sinks in – 3 and 4. The addition of a little dammar varnish to the mixture makes for better handling – 5, 6 and 7

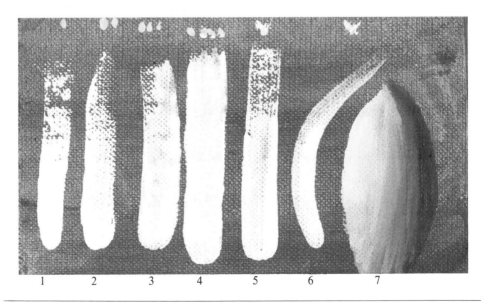

| 1 | 2 | 3 | 4 | 5 | 6 | 7 |

[1] *Stand Oil – Materia Pictoria*, Vol 1 by Hesketh Hubbard, Pitman, 1939.

9 Styles in painting and painting vehicles

Sickert's bogey, the 'linoleum' effect

Linseed oil and turpentine as media have been considered in previous chapters. The question now arises – are more complex media necessary? Resins, gums and balsams have been part of the artist's range of painting materials. They have been used more in the past perhaps, than they are now. Today recently invented alkyd resins have entered the field – how do they fit in with the tradition of painting? Emulsions that blend egg, or gum arabic, or wax with oils, need to be found a place in the development of painting, as well as the resins.

Before the discussion of resin vehicles or emulsions is embarked upon, it is as well to pause and reflect upon the relationship of the painting vehicle to the styles and fashions in painting.

Most people, at the present time, use the simplest things – turpentine or turpentine and linseed oil. Many painters view with distrust anything which involves resins and varnishes. Is this because each painter has chosen that which suits his or her way of painting best, or is it because fashion has pushed the variety of recipes out of favour?

A great deal can be learnt by 'sitting next to Nellie' as the workroom phrase has it. There was a time when, in every studio, the personal choice of each practitioner could be noticed and watched by fellow students. Today there is little scope for this. Without the studio background where it is the practice of students to use a variety of media, you have to 'go it alone' without the useful short cut of picking up tips. It takes a month or so to give a medium a fair trial and so it takes a long time to explore two or three recipes for the contents of the dipper to find out which really suits your kind of painting.

Medieval painters used egg tempera, an excellent and lasting medium – but with limitations. In later medieval times, painters who wanted to explore further took to drying oils (linseed, poppy and walnut).

When you look at the work of Van Eyck and see the solid undeniable presence of *Giovanni Arnolfini and his Wife* painted in 1434 now in the National Gallery, you can see that he made great demands on his medium. It had to convey a powerful sense of reality, solidity and the immediacy of personal contact. This is a field unexplored by tempera painters such as Duccio and Fra Angelico. The Flemish painters like Van Eyck probably used an emulsion of egg and oil. The relevance of such a medium is still valid today.

For a series of mural paintings R T Cowern RA has chosen the use of egg emulsion tempera in which the whole egg/stand oil/a thick dammar varnish/and (soft or distilled) water, are brought together by shaking to make a painting vehicle aptly suited to the form of the painting. In the course of working with this emulsion, Cowern has found that the further addition of an egg *yolk* to the above ingredients is an improvement. The panels, prepared with the traditional gesso ground, has a stippled texture in the intonaco or final coat. This takes the place of the more usual smooth, burnished surface used for smaller panels.

Placed as they are completed on the walls of the refectory of the premises of L G Harris and Co, Ltd, Stoke Prior, Worcester, Brush Manufacturers, the panels are in a high key of colour. The crisp and animated nature of the

A Pigeon Loft 6 ft × 5 ft – 1·83 m × 1·50 m mural panel by R T Cowern ra. The painting is vignetted to within about 4 in. – 12 cm of the limits of the panel. It is to hang in the Refectory of L G Harris & Co, Ltd, Stoke Prior.

One of a series of panels denoting the seasons, now being painted. Some are already in position. For these the artist has chosen a painting vehicle particularly suited to its purpose. High keyed in colour, full of movement and yet crisp in drawing Cowern's painting vehicle which includes the whole egg/stand oil/thick dammar varnish/distilled water/and yet another egg, but the yolk only, shows that the painter, learned in his craft can call on methods from far back in painting history.

Reproduced by courtesy of the artist

The Marriage of Giovanni Arnolfini 32¼ in. × 23½ in. – 81·8 cm × 59·7 cm by Van Eyck, painted 1434. Reproduced by courtesy of the Trustees of The National Gallery, London.

Van Eyck, in this painting shows the solid, undeniable presence of the subject and explored further than the limited field imposed by the medium of egg tempera. He opened up a new world intellectually which his craftsmanship was equal to expressing, by perhaps, taking part in inventing and certainly exploring the new linseed oil based media

27

compositions needs the particular qualities this medium can afford. In the panel here illustrated, *The Pigeon Loft*, light and shade and the cast shadows and the vital movement of flight take an important part in the design. The racing pigeons are very characteristic in attitude and at the same time each feather has its place in mathematical sequence and the dynamic quality of their flight is fully expressed. This is a good example of the experienced painter, Cowern, being able to select from a variety of painting vehicles, the one most appropriate to the work in hand, one with several strata of meaning brought together in harmony.

From the time of Leonardo da Vinci up to the end of the nineteenth century a great many mixed media were evolved in the studios of the masters. The great variety in handling and therefore in texture can be seen in comparing Leonardo and Franz Hals, Constable, with John Singer Sargent. Even a very minor Victorian seascape will have a liveliness of handling which seems to depart with the twentieth century. Look at the blob of paint that makes the highlight on the eye of a Romney portrait or the confluence of two or three brushstrokes that makes the lip moist and alive in a John Phillip portrait of the mid nineteenth century.

Yet today many painters are shy of using more than turps and oil. With turps and oil no painter can guard against parts of the picture sinking in, drying in or producing slippery or leathery parts. Only by very quick methods of work and perhaps with the help of the palette knife does work keep an initial brightness. Little development or working on into wet paint is really possible.

This shyness of complex mixtures in the dipper has an historical origin. It is partly because both the Impressionists in France and the Pre-Raphaelites in England foreswore the browns and shadowy canvasses of the previous generations. They looked for daylight brightness. That, however, does not seem to be the whole story. The Impressionist painting is generally taken for granted to be 'alla prima' – painting in which fresh pigment is applied with no preparation of underpainting.

Examination of some Impressionist pictures shows this to be so, but on the other hand, it seems that a large number of the Impressionists painted in many different ways. A great deal depended on their initial training and even more on their reaction from this training.

That the variety of Impressionist techniques was more or less unexplored territory to the conventional manual on painting methods, was discovered by Bernard Dunstan RA whilst researching for his book on this subject.[1] He found that the methods of the Impressionist painters were complex and diverse.

Another source of information is a literary one, a contemporary writing that gives *another* clue. When reading George Moore's *Conversations in Ebury Street*[2] I came across a verbatim report of a discussion in which there was a powerful deprecation of the use of linseed oil (and presumably all other rich and resinous painting vehicles). George Moore was the friend and confidant of many leading painters. The *Conversations*, gleanings of the period up to its first publication in 1924, seems to have appeared at a very significant date. From that time on many English painters who had worked in a traditional way, changed their tactics. The rich, warm, transparent darks of the past became 'soupy' and were counted symptoms of bad taste.

The light key of the paintings of The Bloomsbury Group were found by some to be desirable. Critics such as Roger Fry had no inhibitions about decrying what they could not cope with themselves and all was not felt to be well at the time when George Moore decided to write.

Walter Richard Sickert, a painter learned in tradition, knowledgeable about painting methods, could use with success quite complicated techniques.[3] He had a wide tone range and varied colour. He was also a bit of a pundit. He tended to lay down the law to his contemporaries and cronies.

Discontent with the Academics and distrust of the progressives made George Moore, P Wilson Steer, Henry Tonks and Professor Brown of the Slade School confer together hoping that Sickert would come back from

George Moore 23¾ in. × 19¾ in. – 60 cm × 50 cm by WALTER RICHARD SICKERT 1860–1942. Reproduced by courtesy of The Tate Gallery, London. The writer, George Moore, kept a very perceptive – if owlish – eye on the movement of the weathercock of art movements during the *'fin de siecle'*. His keen mind behind the rather undecided features inspired in Sickert the intellectual curiosity to make the most perceptive portrait of his painting career

---

[1] *The Painting Methods of the Impressionists* by Bernard Dunstan RA Watson-Guptill Publications, 1976

[2] *Conversations in Ebury Street* by George Moore. First published in a limited edition 1924; 2nd edition 1930

[3] Dunstan p 171

The Slade Professor at The Royal Academy caricature by E HEBER THOMPSON 1923. The caption to the drawing is:
'And I would that my tongue could utter.
The thoughts that arise in me.'
—showing the anguish suffered by Henry Tonks, Slade Professor at the sight of the fashions and factions of the art of his time

the Continent and make some telling pronouncement to deliver art from its condition of schism and disunity.[4]

Tonks relied on his best students in the Slade to continue in the tradition of Turner, Constable and Gainsborough with a thought now and again for Millais and W Holman Hunt.

Perhaps the chief bogey was that some students attempting to emulate John Singer Sargent's orchestrated bravura would, without his finely accurate drawing and his intense power of conception, fall flat on their faces – leaving them in a welter of meaningless oily, leathery paint.

Moore sets the scene. He indicates the disquiet of the New English Art Club and the Slade School. This was in spite of the fact that Tonks was producing very fine painting at the time and P Wilson Steer and others in the New English were setting up a tradition that was to endure until today.

They all awaited Sickert's return. Rumour reached them that Sickert was – 'teaching in Camden Town' – 'at Westminster School of Art' – and 'that he was having an exhibition on a large scale'.

'He cannot paint and draw and teach all day!' cried Tonks.[5] Moore summed up: 'We were all like cattle lowing at the approach of a thunderstorm – At last the crash came. Sickert had brought back a method of painting from France, invented by himself, by means of which an intelligent pupil could be taught to paint.'

'We shall lose half our students' cried Tonks in despair. Brown suggested that they might adopt Sickert's methods.

'But I cannot teach a method in which I don't believe!' exclaimed Tonks. 'I shall resign!!!' In George Moore's style, shot through with irony and satirical hyperbole, he takes it upon himself 'to explain to the reader Sickert's great discovery'. It still remains at this distance of time difficult to visualise what was going to cause Tonks to contemplate instant resignation.

Moore identifies Sickert's method as one which was to enable the pupil to avoid making his painting look like *linoleum*! The situation was that painters like Manet or

---

[4] Moore p 118   [5] Moore p 120

Whistler could paint on and repaint without deterioration.

The inept student, struggling on, would find his canvas getting overloaded and slippery. Later touches would either sink in or stand on top looking alien to the underpainting. It would need a student with a soul of fire to work on past this dread denigration – his work looking like *linoleum* – to work on to the serenity and certaintly of a Van Eyck or the rich complexity of a Rembrandt.

If Tonks himself seemed on the point of being stampeded, it is not surprising that lesser mortals fled to various extremes to avoid the stigma of *linoleum*. Like 'bad taste' any means would be seized upon to avoid it. In Manchester in the 1940s students were mixing handfuls of alabaster with their oil paint and instructors in all sorts of schools were inspired to drive all students to mix white with all their pigments in another bid for good taste. There grew the belief that however bad the drawing, however weak the conception, the picture could somehow be forced externally into a mould of conformity. Many students will have had experiences of having limitations imposed and shibboleths inculcated in lieu of direction towards an objective appreciation of the world around them. The result is that many students work quickly, work 'alla prima', start again rather than develop a theme and are generally denied the full vocabulary of their craft and are therefore limited in the means of expression. Each painter has an individual movement and an individual handwriting. The right medium needs to be found to suit this. A sufficiently wide choice of media must be explored so that one can have some 'play', in the sense of room to manoeuvre and a joyous freedom when you can poise like a ballerina on the point of your paintbrush before executing a *pas de deux* on the canvas.

10 Fat over Lean

A recommended order of procedure towards oil and varnish media

In chapter 9 the workshop was left whilst a visit was made to the library, and George Moore's *Conversations in Ebury Street*, published in 1924, were consulted.

This gave an opportunity to gain, with the rather mischievous but perceptive George Moore, a detached view of what was happening then to artistic fashion.

Many changes of style took place although they did not affect the tradition of painting methods to any measurable degree. The change described by Moore, on the other hand, seems to have had a deep and lasting effect. It is an effect that has largely gone unnoticed; it has been somewhat negative; but we are under its influence today. The 'avant garde' has been so sensational it has masked the small but continuing thread of the tradition of English painting, obscuring its progress.

Sickert decried the use of oil and resin media as producers of 'the linoleum effect' in his student's work – (not in his own!). Of course, patrons as well as students – were frightened off. Nothing much was offered in its place except that a mat finish seemed to be safer and more inclined to avoid errors of taste. Gouache came to the fore and a revival in egg tempera painting was a valuable refreshment to the painter's craft.

Some additions have been evolved to produce a very mat effect such as marble dust. One must note that the mat, opaque picture is rather insistent on its own immediate texture and surface. It lacks the power of the traditional easel picture to take you beyond the surface into the world of its subject. The cause of the neglect of the oil/resin media has not been the media. A neglect of sound drawing embracing the objective knowledge of proportion, scale, anatomy, perspective, light and shade together with a lack of power in the painter's conception are perennial troubles and must be overcome. No amount of linseed oil, copal oil medium or megilp will compensate for weak conception *but* if work is done objectively with the endeavour to express what is understood about the subject of study, *then* it may well be necessary to stretch the technical resources to the full. A variety of media is needed to help in the prodution of the result that belongs to the painter's means of expression.

After this spell on the theories and chapters on the different states of linseed oil, it will now be well to describe the order of some of the practical procedures that can be explored by the painter.

The old adage 'Paint fat over lean', already stated, will now be defined. Fat paint is that which is filled with oil or oil and resin. Lean paint is that in the tube diluted with turpentine (or oil of spike lavender – two evaporating or ethereal oils).

I have elsewhere described painting with a monochrome.[1] If this painting procedure is carried out, the initial painting is with turps only. Even without a full monochrome it is useful to draw the subject in paint to get its placing. Again this will need turps only. This is the 'lean' painting.

Very little turps should be used, pouring out

---

[1]*Leisure Painter*, October, November and December issues 1978, articles by Catherine Moody.

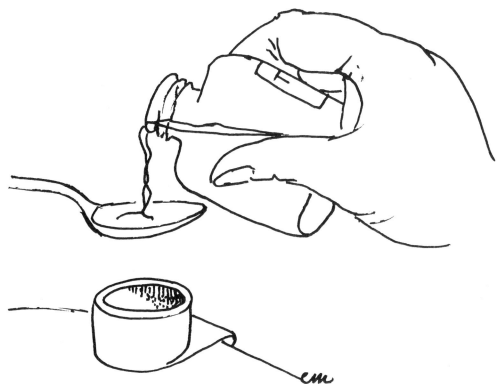

No more than a teaspoonful of turpentine should be poured into the dipper at a time. It is not a good plan to use partly evaporated turpentine

a teaspoonful at a time, as needed. It is not a good plan to use half evaporated turpentine. The bottle must be kept corked tightly and in the dark.

The pigments used for the initial lean painting have significance. Those which have a natural tendency to dry should be chosen. For example raw umber (a cool brown) and cobalt blue are driers. A mixture of ivory black, yellow ochre and a touch of Venetian red, the verdaccio of the early Italians is, like the other earth colours, inert and safe and free from chemical reactions. Terre vert (green earth) gives value to succeeding warm colours. My father, Victor H Moody, uses cobalt blue and light or Venetian red which he says is a somewhat 'jollier' colour than the umber and equally good as a dryer, for his initial lav in.

The turps evaporates quickly and these pigments are natural driers. No added chemical is needed and the lean lay in can be done in a matter of minutes, or if it is desirable it can be worked on for hours.

Next comes the 'build up' with solid impasto and it is technically sound to use the paint from the tube with nothing else. The pigment is ground in ample oil to bind it together. Indeed, the oil in the tube is sometimes excessive. The only turps that is needed is a touch on the tip of the brush so that it holds its shape. On the other hand, the required colour and tone can be mixed and also applied with a palette knife.

It is possible to work like this with solid paint right from the start, assessing colour, tone and drawing all in one go. It is a straightforward way of painting but it means there is much to assess and much to express all at once. This is what many people do today. It ensures brilliance and a spontaneous quality if the painter is fully keyed up by his subject. However, it does not give scope for working on and developing. The initial summing up cannot be further intensified. This is because of physical as well as intellectual reasons. After this stage the surface will be rough and rocky. To make further paint lay on there is a temptation to dilute it with turps and wash it over the existing paint layer, whereupon it will run into the crevices of the impasto. This never looks happy and often results in passages which 'sink in'. becoming dry, mat dull and alien to the rest of the paint. It comes from putting lean turpsy paint over the fat tube paint. The third stage should be increasingly fat.

Two time-honoured additions to the dipper are the sun thickened cold pressed linseed oil and the stand oil which I have described in an earlier chapter. I will now show where they take their place in the procedure of a painting's development.

Both oils are thick and need to be mixed with turps, either 1:1 or 1 oil to two parts turps. Both these media enable paint to be laid on top of the previous paint layer even when it

is wet or half dry. With the medium the pigment does not run away into the grooves; it retains the identity of the brush stroke to a certain extent.

Michael Dinkel RWS, ARCA, RWA, formerly of the Royal College of Art, School of Mural Decoration, speaks affectionately of stand oil: 'It is a beautiful medium. Its qualities are that it stays where you put it and stays brilliant. It lends itself to flower painting giving delicate identity to petal forms.' Its brush strokes are rounded and it is durable. I have found Winsor and Newton's stand oil the best.

Sun thickened oil is quite thick, almost like

Stand oil is very thick. A palette knife must be used to cut off the amount wanted, to stir in the turps and to mix it thoroughly.

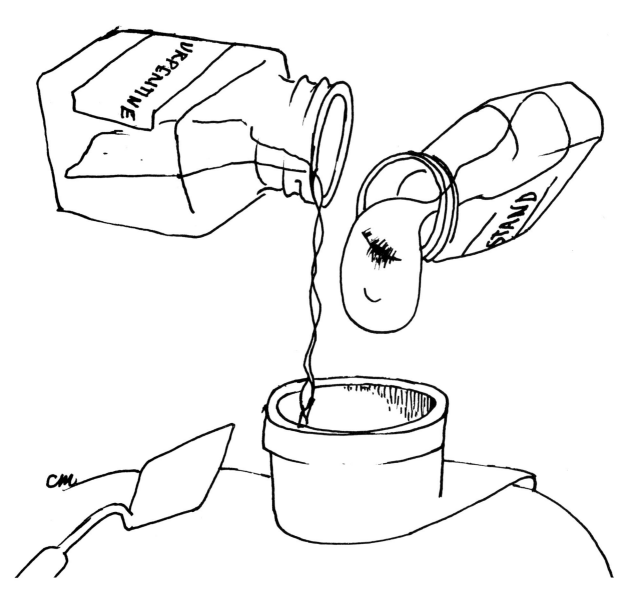

honey; and needs to be mixed with turps. It can be 1:1 or 1 oil to 2 parts turps. The painter's needs dictate the proportion. Sun thickened oil has the advantage of being very pale and blond (when made in one's own garden in a summer of sun.) That which we have made at home has the advantage of remaining pale and it brings the least possible yellowness to delicate pinks or blues.

Both these additions to the dipper enable paint to be applied over previous paint layers, and a further addition of a little dammar varnish will increase this property to an even greater degree.

Dammar should appear white-ish and slightly milky in the bottle. It throws down a sediment and the bottle should be shaken vigorously from time to time. By far the best dammar varnish is produced by Roberson.

With the oil mixture the proportion of dammar would be

2 parts of either sun thickened or stand oil

4 parts turps

1 part dammar varnish

It is a good plan to mix these together and keep them in a small bottle, shaken frequently; only a little is needed in the dipper. Because

Sun thickened cold pressed linseed oil is thick like honey and very blond. Again a palette knife is needed to mix it with the turps. Both these mixtures should only be used *after* the initial stages of the painting

Dammar varnish, oil
and turps together
mixed with the
pigment form the 'fat'
that goes over the
'lean'

there are more ingredients it must not be assumed that *more* medium is needed. The customary amount should be used so that the pigment is not drowned. The proportions can always be altered whilst painting progresses. If it clogs the brush the additions of turps will correct it; if it seems ineffectual add more dammar varnish; if it dries too quickly add oil.

Both these mixtures are media with a flowing 'long' handling quality. Yet, although it enables the brush stroke to go a long way, the paint put on will hold up on top of the previous paint layer. It does not sink in. I think most painters at some time will have come to the point where their efforts to get the paint to go on become ineffectual. The paint is wet and the paint on the brush is as likely to take something off the canvas as to do the other thing. The effort to land a brush load of paint of improved colour or more correct tone on the canvas produces no result. This may be because the whole thing is too wet and soggy. The procedure from lean to fat means that the earlier layer is partly dry and the latest touches of fat pigment will then hold up on top. Because it is on top it will dry easily. If the fat paint was underneath, evaporation and drying would be inhibited. It can even be sealed off – with obviously unfortunate results – because of its need for oxygen and light. Symptoms of the wrong order of the layers are wrinkling or cracking of the paint surface.

These two concoctions give a flowing paint vehicle. They both have a 'long' handling quality. The student needs to be prepared to find that, although it is a nice medium, it is not the one he would choose. It is worthwhile to use it for some time and then its properties can be known in case it is needed for some subject that it would particularly fit.

Every painter needs to find the medium that suits his temperament. Some prefer a 'short' medium with a buttery quality. There are recipes for these too. The exploration does not stop here. Buttery media, emulsions as well as gums and resins are waiting to be investigated.

I might mention one weapon here to combat the 'linoleum' bogey. It is a piece of cuttle-fish bone (as used by cage birds for sharpening their beaks). The oil in the paint layer 'gravitates' to the surface. If this is excessive the picture should be rubbed over, when it is quite dry, with the soft, abrasive, porous side of the bone. When the ensuing white powder is dusted off with a clean, soft rag, the canvas will be found to be more ready to receive further efforts. It will have rubbed off any too impervious skin of dry oil and any too insistent knots and textures and will have made the surface hungry for more paint.

In order to know something of the usage of the present time in studio practice, I have provided students coming to Malvern School of Art with a questionnaire form. The completed forms have produced some useful information and give an idea of the average contents of the dipper.

Most people use turpentine, over half use linseed oil as well, usually mixed with the turps, and one used poppy oil. Of those using turps and paint from the tube, one used white spirit. Some had tried and rejected a number of proprietary brands of medium but one spoke very well of Roberson's medium. A few used Maroger medium. Some, seeking a mat surface or heavy impasto, use gesso, grog, or any white gritty or sandy material. One student, having these additions imposed upon her against her inclinations, had vigorously rejected them!

On the other hand, stand oil had come up from time to time and one student, needing some richness for a black ribbon, had used re-touching varnish. This was originally made of dammar varnish much diluted with turps. Here was an occasion when one of the oil and dammar mixtures I have described above would probably have been more satisfying to use than re-touching varnish. Copal oil medium was listed in the questionnaire and a rare, but time honoured form of linseed oil, black oil, appeared. This was the favoured medium of one student who made his own from the recipe given by Jacques Maroger who attributed its invention to Giorgione (1476/8–1510) – the Italian Renaissance painter.[2] I tested this medium and found its jelly consistency very pleasant to use in spite of its characteristically smoky colour.

From this investigation changes of approach to painting vehicles seem to be indicated. The need to explore and the need for advice and for practical experience were evident. It also showed where traditional practices are continuing and are being proved to be valuable.

[2] *The Secret Formulas and Techniques of the Masters* by Jacques Maroger, Studio 1948, page 160.

11 From oil and resin to mat wax media

Following William Rothenstein's painting development

Some time has now been spent in the workshop looking into the dipper and investigating painting media and vehicles. This has led me to realise more about our present position in regard to painting techniques and the development of painting in England – and the dilemmas of the recent past. Looking into the dipper may seem to be choosing a very small hole through which to view the artistic achievements of the twentieth century, but it gives a revealing view and prevents one from approaching a large subject from too many directions at one time. Those who are painting with oils today have an excellent range of materials to hand. Yet I get the impression that many artists painting now are not taking advantage of the range that is available. If some of the aids to painting are left unexplored there may be an unnecessary uniformity of handling and texture.

In a previous chapter we found George Moore writing rather ironically of the situation about 1913 when Walter Richard Sickert used the derogatory term 'linoleum' to describe the unfortunate appearance of a canvas with a too lavish use of linseed oil. This anecdote, with its entirely negative conclusion has led me to think that this problem – partly aesthetic and partly technical – needs analysis.

One of the most learned painters of the Modern English School, Sir William Rothenstein, showed in his painting a most marked evolution. His work in the 1890s exemplifies the manipulation of flowing pigment and the full tone range of the early tradition.

In the second decade of the twentieth century, in contrast, he began to use a procedure characterised by dry handling and simplicity.

Rothenstein, a thoughtful and knowledgeable painter, knew too much to be affected in the way that George Moore attributes to P Wilson Steer[1] and Henry Tonks. He carved out his own path. As Principal of the Royal College of Art he set a stamp of sincerity and integrity on several generations of students.

He was, as a very young student, familiar with and encouraged by Degas and Toulouse-Lautrec. He had first-hand experience of the main trends of Impressionism. More than most painters he had absorbed a wide range of tradition. From Alfonse Legros,[2] at the Slade School, London, he learnt of the early and high Renaissance roots, working for a year from the antique casts, copying in the National Gallery. He was familiar with the drawings of Raphael, Signorelli, Leonardo and Michelangelo and the Northern men such as Durer and Holbein from the great collections in the British Museum Print Room. His contemporaries were Charles Wellington Furse, P Wilson Steer, Sickert, Orpen and Augustus John and he was set, for all his Parisian experience, firmly in the English tradition.

One of his most memorable paintings, *The Doll's House*, painted in 1899, has a full range of tone with transparent darks and the direct manipulation of the brush which arises from the use of oil or oil and resin/varnish medium.

---

[1] P Wilson Steer, although temporarily dismayed, never deviated from his own method of work.

[2] Alfonse LeGros born 1837, died 1911. Professor of Fine Art at Slade and University College, London, 1876–1892).

An exercise in painting carried out by a student of Malvern School of Art. This copy was made from the original painting by Alfonse LeGros 1837–1911. A study, very likely a demonstration portrait by Legros was lent to the School by The Victoria and Albert Museum. Close scrutiny of the paint structure by the student enabled him to attempt a recapitulation of the painting process from the tinting of the ground to the last brush strokes.

Reproduced by courtesy of William Sly

the time the underlying modelling and characterisation. The exercise in copying here reproduced, by my student, Mr William Sly, was a valuable lesson in methods of painting, but even more, in Bill Sly's words, 'it brought home the speed and certainty that must go along with the painting method, to begin to approach the quality of the original'. It is a pity that we cannot see Legros at work, but the picture itself reveals the fact, recorded by more than one witness, that Legros built up a very complete study in about two hours.[3] With such a method and with the congenial paint vehicle Legros must have chosen, the consideration of drawing, proportion perspective, etc, must have been greatly facilitated by the speed of drying and the ability to work on, without any tendency of the paint to sink in or lose modelling in over-painting. His method and his medium must have meant that a wide range of elements were fully controlled.

With this procedure, Rothenstein was able to record much more than external appearance. There is a living quality in his early self-portraits. Furthermore the quality of life apparent in *The Doll's House*, leads on to a fuller vitality. Association and former experience is drawn upon. The title taken from Ibsen's play allows each spectator to explore for himself the inner meaning beyond the simple elements of the two figures portrayed and the light and shade which evokes thought and feeling.

Later Rothenstein relinquished this field of activity with its scope for complexity. He changed to the use of much drier paint built up without flowing strokes. The portrait *Eli, The Thatcher* painted in 1913 is redolent of the simplicity of the life of a Cotswold craftsman. The tone range of the portrait is limited; there are no really dark tones. The surface is mat and the gently modelled form is built up with an almost stippled impasto. This probably needed no medium beyond the oil in the tube.

At this time the Arts and Crafts Movement was bringing architects and designers back to an appreciation of the natural qualities of wood, stone and thatch. Artists turned from

(See colour plate facing page 73.) Even earlier his self-portrait of 1890, when he was eighteen, is full of rich colour and the vitality which arises from a dense but almost calligraphic brushwork in the impasto of the lights.

In his autobiography *Men and Memories*, Rothenstein describes how Legros painted a demonstration portrait. He gives details of the procedure: '. . . Beginning by brushing in the shadows, then the half tones, finally adding the broad lights.'

I am familiar with the results of this method of working, for we have had, on loan from the Victoria and Albert Museum, just such an original demonstration portrait by Legros. With the students of Malvern School of Art, who copied the Legros, we have followed, step by step, the process of painting, endeavouring to recapitulate every stage from the toning of the canvas to the final build up of the impasto lights. We used, as far as possible, the same pigments and medium; the aim was to follow through the speed and the movement of the original brushwork – having in mind all

---

[3] The diary *'Rummyniscences' of Thomas William Cole* was privately published by his grandson in 1974. Cole, who became Headmaster of Ealing School of Art, trained at the South Kensington Schools (later to become The Royal College of Art) gives a vivid account of life in The Schools and includes a full description of a visit by Legros to demonstrate before the students, his method of painting a head of oils – 'which was a thing he could do to perfection,' was Cole's comment.

Eli, The Thatcher Oil 30 in. × 25 in. – 75 cm × 63·5 cm by WILLIAM ROTHENSTEIN. Reproduced by courtesy Sir John Rothenstein, OBE, KCStG, Mr Michael Rothenstein, ARA, and The Rutherston Collection, Manchester.
   As compared with the earlier works, the tone range is now limited. The fluent brush work is now gone and the gently modelled form is built up with an almost stippled impasto

Left *Self Portrait* Oil 11 in. × 9½ in. – 27·5 cm × 24 cm) by WILLIAM ROTHENSTEIN. Reproduced by courtesy Sir John Rothenstein, OBE, KCStG, Mr Michael Rothenstein, ARA and The Graves Art Gallery, Sheffield.
   This is a fragment of a larger canvas damaged in the blitz. It exhibits the grace and ease of his early period. Painted *c* 1890

all that characterises the artificialities of urban life. Rothenstein expressed this in his modestly but sensitively conceived picture. With it he takes us from one world to another in painting.

Sir John Rothenstein in his book *Modern English Painters*, speaks of a time of change in his father, Sir William's work: 'Soon after the beginning of the new century a radical change involving both loss and gain began to be manifest in his work.'

It seems evident that the change from the early method of painting to that used in *Eli, the Thatcher* was not accidental. On his return from Paris, William Rothenstein's words were: 'My sympathies were all with realism.'

Approaching the subject of the development of English painting from this narrowest of aspects – the painting medium – it seems to me that the change from fluent to dry handling is not without significance, particularly for those who are looking at the scene from the studio workshop point of view. Does it not seem that, without words, the painter's hand moved from the confident fluency of the nineteenth century to a drier, more controlled medium for the doubts of the twentieth century? Now with hindsight we can see how the major part of the artistic arena has been filled with the activities of the *avant garde*. The progress of the realist and the representational painter has been so much over-shadowed that it has been difficult to discern his progress, or find any coherence or common ground shared by individuals.

William Rothenstein must have foreseen this situation at an early stage. For some, like Pierre Bonnard and Rothenstein's pupil, Edward Le Bas, the path taken was a continuance of the French Impressionist idiom; but for those working in England, many separate paths have been taken. However it is enlightening to see what grew from the dry simplicity that Rothenstein chose in 1913.

Instead of the flowing quality of oil and resin media, the more mat surface of wax comes to hand. Wax is an enduring unchanging material, almost impervious to atmospheric impurity. It has been used in painting from Greco–Roman times.

An important scheme of mural painting was commissioned in the late 1920s. St Stephen's Hall in the Houses of Parliament was decorated with a number of panels illustrating events in English history with emphasis on our development from an Island Kingdom to a worldwide Commonwealth. Rothenstein's subject was *Sir Thomas Roe at the Moghul Court, 1614*. As well as the subject, the colour scheme was specified. All the panels were to harmonise with Michelangelo's *Entombment* in the National Gallery.

Here was an application that was in accord with the approach and method that he had

Sir Thomas Roe at The Moghul Court, 1614. Mural panel in St Stephen's Hall in The Palace of Westminster, canvas 10 ft × 14 ft 6 in. – 3 m × 4·4 m by WILLIAM ROTHENSTEIN. Reproduced by courtesy the Rt Honourable Mr Speaker, House of Commons.

The harmony of the Eastern colour scheme, the detail of the costume and the delicacy of the drawing, bear witness to the value of the wax medium used. Rothenstein's knowledge of Moghul illumination and traditions, with his breadth of compositional power, make this panel a memorable landmark in twentieth-century painting

already developed. The tall, rather narrow Hall demanded a mat surface to avoid viewing the panels being made difficult by shine and reflection. The limited tone range and the simplicity of the compositional form Rothenstein had already discovered. It was already to hand and lent itself to the narrative and historical subject. The panel was completed in 1926. In the tradition of the Renaissance studio, assistants took part in the work. One was Michael Dinkel, Instructor in the School of Mural Decoration of the Royal College of Art of which Sir William was then Principal. There were others such as James Tucker, a student, who worked out the whole of the measured perspective of the composition. Michael Dinkel, in a recent conversation with me on the work done at that time, recalled the wax medium they used from tubes. The Right Hon Percy Grieve, Member for Solihull, who knows this painting well, says that the colour is, even now, bright and very fresh in appearance. Over 50 years has proved the reliability of the wax medium. In 1931 Sir William said that the limitations and rigid specifications that were imposed on all the artists who decorated the St Stephen's Hall panels, so far from being a handicap, were found to form a structure that helped them considerably.

Nineteen thirty one seems a very long time ago and yet it is only now that those of us who choose to paint representationally can feel that we can see the way ahead a little more clearly.

I have traced this development in Sir William Rothenstein's work a little way because I think it shows that when a painter knows the precise demands of the task he has before him, and when his knowledge of painting methods is wide, he can choose the technique most apt for the work and which suits his own painterly language. The result is that a timeless and universal meaning is conveyed that can be comprehended over the years.

12 How to prepare wax media and picture wax for preserving pictures

After a tour of exploration the reader may now like to consider the practical means of preparing further media and gather a recipe for making bees' wax medium. Having found that the neglect of the rich and fluent resins and oils of the eighteenth and nineteenth centuries stems from fashion rather than through any difficulty in finding a variety of painting vehicles, the preparation of a mat surface medium will now follow.

In Chapter 11 it was seen that William Rothenstein moved in his own work from a fluid medium to the use of dry paint with an almost crumbly surface. He also made use, for the special purpose of mural painting, of the almost mat texture of a wax medium.

This is easy to make and is a permanent and unchanging material. Bees' wax does not darken or become yellow with time. It is less likely to darken than linseed oil. Dissolved in genuine turpentine or in white spirit it can be used with oil paint. Too much must not be used because the degree to which wax hardens is less than the hardness of thoroughly dried linseed oil or a good quality resin. However, used with oil paint from the tube the mixture is not likely to become over waxy.

A portrait painted by Victor H Moody in 1920, still in good condition, shows the qualities of wax. The dark tones, where a fair amount of wax medium must have been used, are free from cracks or any distortion. The head in contrastingly pale tones has remained true in colour. The pale flower-like complexion shows no sign of yellowing over the period.

To make wax medium a heavy based saucepan with upright sides is needed. A cylindrical saucepan is a great help for

Mrs Victor Moody by Victor H. Moody. Oil and wax 24 in. × 20 in. – (62 cm × 50 cm). Painted with wax medium. The dark tones which must have contained a fair amount of this medium are in a good state of preservation. The strongly contrasting pale flower-like tones of the head are in equally good condition, showing no colour change over a period of many years

Diagram showing the use of the card marked in intervals to measure the proportion of melted wax to turpentine or white spirit. A proportion of two parts wax to four or five parts of fluid gives a useful consistency. Less than four parts leaves the wax too hard to use. If you need a very fluid medium up to six parts of fluid can be mixed. For extra safety a double saucepan may be used

measuring. This can be done fairly accurately in the saucepan. (Decanting into other vessels leads to great difficulties.) As the inflammable ingredients, wax and turpentine, will be warmed precautions must be taken. The mixture **must not** be heated over an open flame; a closed range, old-fashioned coal or the modern equivalents. I use a Rayburn cooker. For extra safety use a double saucepan with a water holding base as used for boiling milk. This recipe is however actually safer than frying chips. The temperature

needed is much lower than that needed for fish frying.

In recipes for making wax preparations directions are often given to grate up the bees' wax before melting. This is a very tiresome chore and quite unnecessary. Simply put the lumps of wax in the saucepan and heat very gently on the stove. Allow the amount needed to melt off the lump and then remove the now diminished lump from the saucepan with a pair of sugar tongs. This can cool on a tin lid before being put away. In the pot the melted wax will be in a fluid state. It should be taken off the heat for the next stage. A strip of thin card needs to be ready cut beforehand. A handy size is about $1\frac{1}{2}$ in. by 9 in. – 3·5 cm by 22·5 cm long. This is a measure for quantities. Place it perfectly upright in your melted wax; hold it steady for a few moments for the wax to soak in to the card to show its depth. Take this distance and mark off three equal intervals up the edge of the card. Now with the saucepan still off the stove, have the turps ready. Replace the card upright in the pot and pour in sufficient turps to fill it up to the second mark making a proportion of 1 wax to 1 turps. This makes a fairly stiff medium. If you would like it more fluid fill it up to mark $2\frac{1}{2}$ or 3. The latter gives a fairly fluid medium of 1 wax to 2 turps. Stir and if the cold turps solidifies the wax, return to a gentle heat and continue stirring until the wax melts. Remove from the heat immediately and continue to stir gently until it cools a little. Then, before it solidifies, pour into clean screw top jars.

For this painting medium artist's distilled turpentine should be used. To make a handy amount use a $4\frac{1}{2}$ in. – 11·5 cm width saucepan; the wax should be melted to a depth of $\frac{1}{2}$ in. – 1·5 cm.

The medium is added to the oil paint whilst working, remembering that the more medium added, the more transparent the paint becomes. Do not expect to obliterate any dark faulty painting that is unwanted. If it is wrong, scrape it off, before painting again.

Picture wax used as a protective coating for a painting is very useful. Prepare in the same way as the medium using the proportion 2:3 wax to turps. Any oil painting is the better for a coat of varnish about six months after it has been painted. Before varnishing, dust the painting completely with dry cotton wool. Use a number of small pellets of cotton wool

Top: brush strokes of raw umber with wax medium
Below: brush strokes of flake white with wax medium.
In both cases the medium was in the proportion 1:2, wax to turps

and throw each one away as it becomes soiled. Then remove any lint with a clean linen rag and the palm of a clean hand. Then varnish with a good picture varnish. After about two weeks when the varnish is quite dry, lightly rub over the picture with 2 to 3 parts mixture using a linen rag to apply it. Allow it to dry for three minutes and then rub over with a clean cloth to distribute the wax and polish the surface. If you do not want a highly polished surface, the use of white spirit will ensure a slightly mat finish. If a more polished surface is desired, use distilled turpentine for the picture wax as you did for the wax medium. Speed is essential when the wax is applied, but also a light hand. Slow, hard rubbing may dissolve the paint; if there is an area of a strong colour – for instance a red jumper in a portrait – this must be watched. See that the red is not rubbed into the delicate colour of the head and neck. This caution also applies to the application of varnish. Scarlet lake is a pigment very prone to 'bleed' in these conditions. Paint with the turpentine mixture as it combines best with the pigment. Use white spirit in the mixture for coating the picture as it is less prone to mix.

Ready made wax preparations are available. There is an Opal medium which contains 5% wax and Winton matt varnish is rendered mat by the use of wax.

Rowney's Matwax is designed to give a mat finish to a completed oil painting.

None of these picture wax preparations should be applied *before* varnishing – always afterwards – as a protective coat. A rub over with cotton wool every two months will keep the picture surface fresh and alive. A picture that has been kept in store and is looking rather dead and neglected will respond to this treatment of a dry clean with cotton wool, varnishing and then dressing with picture wax, and henceforth a regular dusting and an occasional additional light coat of picture wax.

A picture painted with wax medium does not need varnish at all. Picture wax is sufficient and varnish would provide an intrusive layer of a different degree of hardness.

Another very permanent way of using wax is the encaustic painting of the Greco–Roman–Egyptian period. Portraits of the deceased painted on coffin lids in the second and third centuries AD are splendid and well preserved examples of this art. They can be seen in the British Museum and the National Gallery. Here the dry, ground pigment seems to have been combined with the melted wax and laid in with heated palette knives. It is an enduring method and was used most dextrously. However, I have never come across anyone practising this method today and it occurs to me that the hotter Mediterranean climate may be a necessary ingredient in this technique.

The use of bees' wax I have described is not the encaustic method since it depends on turpentine, not heat, to make the solid wax usable. Bees' wax can be obtained from the chemist or from bee-keepers. Agricultural and flower shows often have a section on bee-keeping and provide a good opportunity to contact the producers of wax. Pale colour wax is best for the painter. The darker wax can be made into an excellent furniture polish, using the same proportion 2 wax to 3 turps and adding a teaspoonful of linseed oil.

The Pheasant by Catherine Moody (detail)
Actual size of the pheasant's head about 4½ in. (11 cm). This shows the glazing of the highly coloured wattle round the beak and eye. Both vermilion and ultramarine were used in several degrees of tone. Glazing avoided interaction between vermilion and lead white – see figure 45 – and with both pigments gave the advantage of the optical qualities of transmitted light. If the vermilion had been mixed directly with white it would have produced a pink. Various tones of vermilion were the pheasant's colouring and no pink was evident in the high keyed colour
See also figure 49 and page 68

13 Resin painting vehicles (A)

Having described the use of turpentine and linseed oil in its various forms, I am now moving on to the mixed media which contain resins. Some of these are semi-solid (creamy or buttery) and are supplied in tube form.

The consideration of the medium is indivisible from the painter's intention and aims. It is closely linked to the philosophy of art.

However, the search for the medium that suits his way of painting can be an unconscious quest on the part of the artist. The medium or vehicle should be a means of liberating him from difficulties or handicaps, such as paint drying slowly when the painter needs to push on with the work, or the mixing of normally incompatible pigments. Tempo and temperament also come into the field of exploration.

Firstly if we consider tempo, some artists work at speed, others wish to paint deliberately. On the whole the worker who likes to dash off a painting on the spot from a subject, and aims for the qualities of directness and spontaneity, encounters few technical problems. The paint from the tube is usually equal to this sort of demand. On the other hand if, in Bernard Dunstan's words, there is the wish 'to dig deeply in a chosen field of painting',[1] ie those who want to work with repeated sittings of the model, or numerous painting sessions on the more durable still life subject – it will be found that a more sophisticated medium than the simple turpentine dilution is needed.

A painter 'working on' with such a simple medium will find that subsequent layers will 'sink in'. In this condition the paint surface

The Pugin Drawing-Room at Eastnor Castle by Catherine Moody (detail)
The colour scheme of this interior of Pugin's recalled an earlier period than that in which he was working. A link with Nash and the designs of Brighton Pavilion was found to connect the two otherwise dissimilar buildings. Blues and pinks and gilding were the key-notes in common. The blue in the ceiling set off the rosy pink of the pure silk damask curtains. Though the textile was old, the colour gleamed with a pure rosiness. This took many mixings of the many reds available to the artist's palette, before the right tints were discovered. The folds of the curtains received direct light on a very limited area. To make sure that the colour was sustained, a build up of white impasto was established where the sunlight fell and the pigment was carried over it in a glaze medium. Only thus could a sufficiently glowing tint be achieved
See also figure 51

---

[1] Introduction to the course in Representational Painting, from 'Life at Malvern School of Art', demonstrator Bernard Dunstan RA.

Resin painting vehicles (a)

A bowl quickly painted with a few strokes. The proportion and shape is indicated. Oil paint on canvas 5 in. × 4 in. − 12·5 cm × 10 cm

The painting taken further so that the shape and quality of the bowl begins to be realised. Oil paint with a resin medium

dries unevenly, the painting loses its unity, and painstaking modelling will get lost.

The painting gets most 'out of key' when it is half dry and this is when the consideration of the next step concerns the artist most deeply. If the canvas could dry for three weeks between each stage it would be found that the painting regained its unity as it became thoroughly dry. However, it is difficult to sustain one's thread of thought with this attenuated plan of painting. The practical difficulty of keeping the subject to hand, whether a portrait or a bottle and a loaf, over a prolonged period, is often an insuperable one. It is necessary therefore to explore the resinous vehicles to see if they can offer some quality that will help to sustain freshness and unity to the conception as it grows on the canvas.

If, for instance, work is being done on a still life study that includes a pottery bowl, a swift impression might be achieved by dashing in an ellipse for the rim, a graduated shadow on the dark side, and a facet of high keyed impasto for the plane facing the light. If the picture is to be developed it will be necessary to paint numerous touches surrounding that facet, to break down the plane to something approaching the curve of the surface of the bowl. As the development of the picture proceeds, the later touches need to stand up and remain pure in colour and retain their brushwork and texture. The aim is to avoid the later paint layer literally 'sinking in' and gravitating towards the canvas through the half wet under-layer of paint.

I am assuming that in doing this the painter is bringing to bear a systematic understanding of light and shade; that he is seeking to depict the impact of light rays on a curved surface. He must have a feeling for the difference between the light rays that hit the bowl at right angles, on the interior or the exterior, and on the rim – and the rays that are tangent to the curves that hit the surface most slantingly, both on the inside and the outside, and on the rim of the bowl.

Thus the surface of the bowl is modelled and the actual shape is built up. Once the shape of the bowl is established, its position in space and the feeling of atmosphere around it can be explored. Surface texture and colour follow this. All this study of the actual formation is termed 'drawing' whether it is

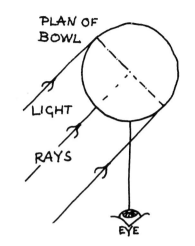

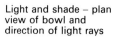

Light and shade – plan view of bowl and direction of light rays

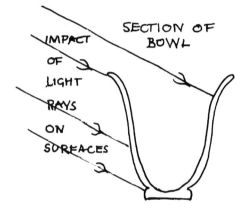

Light and shade – section of the same bowl showing impact of light coming from a high window

done with a pencil or in paint. This way a great deal more information is put down on canvas than is done in a first 'impression'. More important is the fact that the painter is, all the time, developing a fuller understanding of the objects before him.

I interpolate this passage on drawing to make the point that this stage of painting progresses to the consideration of the wholeness of the conception. It may seem a little overpowering to tackle light and shade, perspective, aerial perspective (ie atmosphere), texture and colour in this analytical way, but by this method these problems can be approached one at a time, gradually. The painter is not overwhelmed by dealing with the whole thing in one stroke with no second chance. Resin media are brought in to facilitate this more deliberate advance.

To avoid any misapprehension it must be

clearly understood that the use of resin media is not intended for a quick and easy method for reaching a high degree of finish without the needed analysis of the subject to reach that condition. Let no one imagine that the use of a resin vehicle is a way to facilitate an unthinking licking of the paint surface into smoothness, or a mechanical technique for adding 'shading' to a flat two dimensional conception.

Nothing can take the place of a scientific analysis of where a shadow can or cannot fall.

Those of us who enjoy the painting of the

Crinum in The August Garden Oil painting 9 in. × 7 in. − 22·5 cm × 17·5 cm by CATHERINE MOODY. Maroger medium was used to facilitate continuous painting whilst the lily like blooms retained their shape

masters of the past realize that the qualities of their paintings arise from the underlying accumulation of knowledge about their subject matter, not from any trick of paint manipulation. Their paintings look different from the simply stated impression of today's tyro, not because the paint is different, but because it is the perception behind each brush stroke that impels the painter's movement. To achieve this without handicap these painters sought a medium that could sustain a greater injection of information and study than the plain tube paint.

I have surveyed this field of action rather widely. Because of its nature it is less familiar than 'alla prima' painting. We have all done more quick studies than complex works sustained over a long period.

The Maroger medium supplied by Roberson, in a semi-solid tube has become the one I favour for my own work. It is made to the formula of Jacques Maroger formerly of the Laboratory of the Louvre Museum, Paris. It gives a short and buttery quality to the paint. It accelerates the drying and the brush stroke holds its shape; there is no tendency to flow. Indeed its lack of flow would make it unacceptable to some painters. A flowing medium is described in Chapter 6. It can be achieved by mixing sun thickened cold pressed linseed oil with dammar varnish and best turpentine.

Jacques Maroger in his book on the techniques of the old masters describes in detail the boiling of linseed oil with litharge (protoxide of lead) and maintains that this was the basis of oil painting from its earliest beginnings. The purest form of lead white, basic carbonate of lead is equally used as a drying agent. It is obtainable from Winsor and Newton, under the name of Cremnitz White. Its drying powers are apparent because if the tube is not used up quickly it is apt to become rather solid.

The boiling process converts the oil and the lead to what is known as black oil. It has a smoky appearance rather like the semi-precious stone, the cairngorm. Using some prepared by one of my students I found it quite easy to allow for the lowering of tone in all but the lightest tints. Its texture in handling I found most agreeable. I still prefer Maroger medium which contains, as well as the drying oil, a gum which seems to further improve the handling qualities and also protects the pigment. I have never been troubled by its darkening and a sunfilled landscape which I painted with this medium in the 1940s shows no sign of change.

The lily like flower I painted recently, *Crinum in the August Garden* needed continuous painting for some hours on three consecutive days. The many colours in the white of the strongly curving petals, the fall of the sunlight were not things to be dashed in quickly. Painting all this step by step brought out the full qualities of the medium. It allowed me to 'paint on' without the paint getting soggy painting 'wet into wet' and on the last day the paint strokes were holding up on top of the previous paint without difficulty. The amount of medium I use is about 2 parts of Maroger to 3 parts of flake white mixed together with the palette knife when I first set my palette. This is enough to influence all the colours and tones mixed with white. I then put a squeeze of the medium next to the dipper and mix it with the dark tones and strong colours where none of the white is used. For this I use the brush to mix. In the dipper there is about a teaspoonful of English distilled turpentine, replenished occasionally.

A similar vehicle, Roberson's medium, is recommended by a student who made a practice of using it. Professor Church wrote in its favour in 1901 – 'Roberson's medium has now been in use for something like 60 years. It has been a favourite vehicle with many distinguished artists.[2] It seems that it could be said that it has stood the test of time.[3]

In the next chapter I will list the most useful resins giving their qualities. Anyone wishing to widen the scope of his painting will see that it is worth while to test some new media and perhaps thereby find something that will open up a new phase of individual exploration in painting.

---

[2] CHURCH, A H, *The Chemistry of Paints and Painting*, published 1901, page 121.

[3] *Life and Letters of Millais* by his son. Millais (after 1850) used Roberson's medium. Volume II, page 340.

A petal shape
indicated with a
limited number of
brush strokes.
4 in. × 3 in. –
10 cm × 7·5 cm

The full complexity of
the curves explored
more fully involving
working on for a
longer time. Without a
resin medium the paint
becomes soggy and
difficult to handle.
5 in. × 4 in. –
12·5 cm × 10 cm

14 Resin painting vehicles (b)

Part of the story of resin media was discussed in the last chapter and the description of further examples follows.

In the first part of the twentieth century it began to be unusual for the artist to spend a long time on a painting. Nineteenth century painters expected to sustain their attention over quite a long period and it is known that such a painting as Manet's *La Servante de Bocks*, 1878–9, was worked on over a long series of sittings. The knowledge and power to do this, possessed by most artists before had, by the 1930s, become dissipated.

Often at the outset of painting directly from a subject all goes well until there is an urge to elaborate a certain statement or correct a passage of drawing. The next day you find that the part on which you have worked with most concentration has 'sunk in', gone dull and lost the impact that it had in the first lay-in. This is about the most discouraging thing that can happen to a painter and it is a strong factor in inhibiting further development. Fostering the value of the accidentals of the first touches becomes a barrier to intellectual grasp. It is the resin media that can lift the painter over this style.

The three things desirable in a resin or gum is that it should be as colourless as possible, durable and not inclined to crack or bloom.

Dammar resin and gum arabic are fairly colourless. Mastic resin is pale but is not very durable. Fossil copal resin is golden amber and is wonderfully durable but at present is unobtainable except in a very dark tone. The discovery of an old stock of copal that is amber colour would be a fortunate stroke of luck and should be made use of. Venice turpentine, a semi-solid, is useful but I have not been sure of getting samples that do not darken and so have stopped using it. The following recipe has been used for at least four portraits in our studio with success. The Venice turpentine sample was reliable in the 1960s. All the portraits are in good condition with no darkening over a period of 15 years. The proportions used were as follows:

1 fluid oz of dammar varnish

4 fluid oz of English distilled turpentine

1 fluid oz of Venice turpentine

2 fluid oz of sun thickened CPLO

All the ingredients should be put in a glass jar (preferably screw top). The jar (with the lid off) is then placed in a pan of warm water which can be warmed up on a stove. The mixture is stirred and warmed until the Venice turpentine ceases to be solid and mixes completely with the other ingredients. The minimum amount of heat should be used to mix thoroughly. Too much heat drives off the lighter essences of turpentine and leaves a sticky medium. When it is cool the top is screwed on securely so that the medium can be shaken fairly vigorously before use.

Resins are dissolved in turpentine as a rule and are then mixed with linseed oil. The quality required in the linseed oil is that it should dry reasonably quickly. The preparation of sun thickened cold pressed linseed oil is described in Chapter 6 and is ideal for this recipe as well as for using with turps alone.

If a chemical drying agent is used it should not darken the oil unduly. A typical lead drying agent is litharge. It has this effect to some extent. Its tendency to lower the tone of the paint must be balanced against the usefulness of its quicker drying qualities. The drying oils such as linseed oil and the ethereal oils such as turpentine or lavender oil are both needed in diluting the resins. Some, such as Maroger medium, contain a gum which is incorporated in an emulsified form. The range is quite great when it includes those which stem from tempera painting and use the emulsion of egg yoke, as well as a gum such as gum arabic which dissolves in water and is bonded with the oil and resin in an emulsion. These blendings and mixings have been developed because of their excellent handling qualities.

Many useful media are supplied ready made and it is not necessary for the painter to embark on complicated processes but it is interesting to know a little of what goes on in the back room.[1]

Megilp was a medium familiar to artists in the late nineteenth century. It is a blend of mastic resin and linseed oil. I have come across old tubes of megilp which always seem to be sticky and oozy.

It happens less often now but when I was a student, an elderly amateur would pass on his or her equipment. In this way one was set up with a palette with a beautiful polish, a sketching umbrella with a wealth of clamps and swivels or a paint box of finely grained wood abounding with brass rachets, hooks and locks. In these boxes there were tubes of paint – some too hard to use, others whose labels were so obscure that it was impossible to tell the name of the colour. Often there was a tube oozing a sticky golden fluid that glued it closely to the bottom of the box. You prized it off and scrutinising the print on the now transparent label it was discerned to be marked MEGILP. Why megilp of this era seemed to be never drying I do not know. Perhaps the necessary drying agent was omitted at one time. Strange additions such as quicklime appear in Fairholt's definition of around 1880 along with his firm warning against its use. Winsor and Newton now list megilp amongst their products, and give its ingredients – lead driers, linseed oil, gum mastic and turpentine. It is described in their catalogue as a thin, quick drying jelly medium, amber in colour. I am sure that this firm could produce a thoroughly reliable medium that would be a satisfactory drier with probably

better ingredients than the older recipes. The chief disadvantage of this medium is that the gum mastic used is one of the less durable resins. It is probably for that reason that Winsor and Newton now supply Win-Gel in which alkyd resin is used to make a modern alternative to megilp. This seems to be a useful addition to the list of painting vehicles.

One of my students has prepared the Black Oil, said to be the medium of the early period of oil painting. Another enterprising student, William Sly, has made and used the traditional megilp, dissolving the mastic in turpentine and boiling linseed oil in an enamel vessel with litharge. This process conjures up the vision of the Medieval alchemist at work. It involves heating the oil, an emission of evil smelling smoke and considerable masses of froth. Mixing the liquids together he produced the characteristic jelly medium. Not only was it jelly but also it was thrixotropic. A sharp tap on the vessel containing it turned the mixture to liquid; a few minutes interval and it resumed its jelly like solidity. He found painting with this mixture completely satisfactory, its handling quality being very good.

This thrixotropic quality has the advantage that when you place your brush stroke on the canvas, it stays put and does not subside or flow. On the other hand I find the fact you have to use your brush rather strenuously to mix the pigments and medium slightly impeding. It is probably a help to do some of the initial mixing with a palette knife as one does with Maroger medium. I think this is a help in using Win-Gel.

Another medium dating from 1850–1880 used by many artists is a mixture of copal varnish and poppy oil thinned down after inspissation with oil of spike lavender. Pictures painted with this were recorded as sound, bright and pure in colour as when they were first painted, after an interval of 70 years.

Dame Laura Knight described to me her own method of painting. It is completely direct. In her phrase it was 'Finish as you go, with no second thoughts'. On the other hand Dame Laura described her husband Harold Knight's procedure as one in which he built up the painting bit by bit, going over and over the work. He began with turps and linseed oil

---

[1] Painters wishing to make up a medium can obtain resins from L Cornelissen and Son who stock the raw materials.

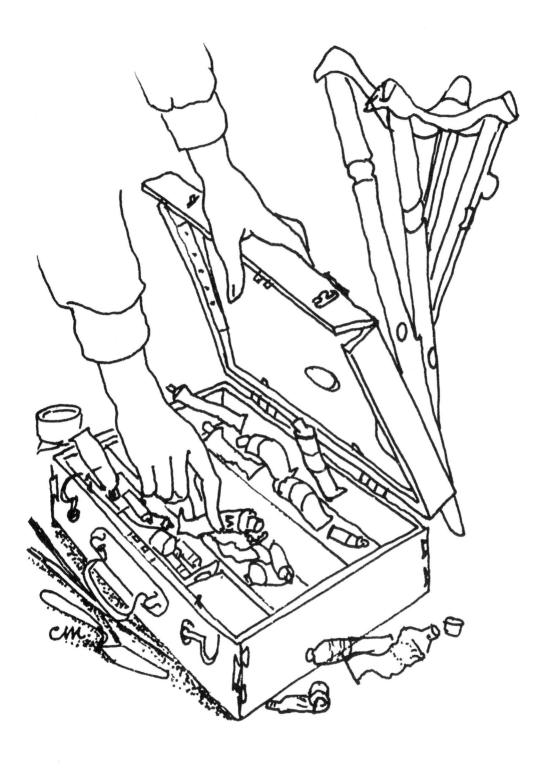

Sometimes an elderly amateur would pass on useful equipment – a paint-box of finely grained wood abounding with brass rachets, hooks and locks. Often at the bottom of the box was a tube oozing a sticky golden fluid that glued it to the box. Often it was a tube of megilp and, as would be expected, used a resin towards the end. 'Last of all he used to add a few drops of amber varnish,' Dame Laura said. Amber, the hardest of all the resins is very rarely used and it is interesting that the special quality of Harold Knight's work arose in some degree from this unusual medium.

For many years I have had hanging on the wall of my room a portrait by John Phillip RA 1817–1867. The inscription at the foot of the canvas reads, 'Painted by John Phillip RA when visitor to the Painting School 1863'. [2] It would seem likely that this was a demonstration done by Phillip for the students of the Royal Academy Schools as the Visitor. The painting is a most valuable teaching aid and I have made a study of it with many students. It shows its method of painting almost as clearly as if one was watching Phillip at work. This is a good example of a painting developed to quite a degree of complexity with the aid of a resin vehicle. Obviously painted quickly, the artist painted wet into wet. After a broad lay-in with a monochrome he worked on until he reached a point where single telling touches made the foundational work come alive. The deft application of a stroke of opaque pink gives the facet of the lower lip. A green blue light shows the transparency of the iris of the eye, and that is made fully comprehensible by the corresponding highlight on the eye. With the built up impasto of the forehead and the painting of detail, the direction of light from a high studio window is revealed.

It is freely and dextrously painted and Phillip laid brushstroke over brushstroke, retaining the calligraphic vigour of his handiwork and the full value of every degree of colour. With turpentine alone the latter part of the painting would have sunk in to the initial broad brushwork. The resin vehicle was the means by which he reached this interesting and unified statement.

These are some of the chief painting vehicles and each painter needs to explore to find which suits him the best. Indeed, tests for permanence and durability, for drying, darkening and cracking should be made at the outset, whatever the source of the materials. An area of the two, three or four painting vehicles should be painted out on glass; the outside of a jam jar is handy. Then the date of the experiment, the names of the media and the recipes and the source of the materials are recorded and the written data can be kept inside the jam jar. The jar should be put on a window sill and looked at from time to time, over a period of three months. If the samples show no deterioration a start can be made in using them, but the tests must be kept indefinitely to refer to at any time. Dammar varnish, copal oil medium, mastic varnish and Maroger medium could be a first set of tests.

It is essential that each painter tries out the feel of a new medium. The application of paint is a very personal thing, as personal as one's handwriting and as little to be disguised as one's walk.

In this chapter I have discussed medium in relation to the full development of painting which has a traditional and objective outlook. Vehicles which can facilitate the use together of incompatible pigments need consideration next and with this the use of resins in the application of glazes.

---

[2] The inscription written with a pointed paint brush at the foot of the canvas below the study is signed *A L Herford*. I had assumed that this was someone in charge of the students whilst the Academician was at work on the demonstration. Miss Constance-Anne Parker, Librarian of the Royal Academy has kindly investigated this question for me. She has found that the only A L Herford on the Royal Academy School's books at that time was Anne Laura Herford, the first girl student. Legend says that she sent in her work under initials only and the powers that be did not realise that she was a girl until she turned up on the first day of term. After that, girls were allowed as students.

It seems that it might have been a kindly compliment to the enthusiastic girl student that John Phillip presented her with the fruits of his session of intensive painting, done under the eyes of one who was ready to absorb and to learn.

Head of a Girl Painted by JOHN PHILLIP RA in 1863. She has long hair, black velvet bands at her neck and wrists and is supporting her head on her hand. Painted as a demonstration, Phillip carried the study to a major degree of complexity and sensitivity of form and colour, yet retained the unity of the whole

Painted by John Phillip R.A.
when visitor in the Painting School '/63
A Notherford

Detail of the lower part of the face revealing every stage of the artist's progress from the broad lay-in to the opaque touch of pink that gives the facet of the lower lip and the luminous and transparent light or Venetian red of the shadow under the nose and the indication of the nostril

Detail
To range from the loose thin underpainting to the built up impasto of the forehead and the fine detail
of the transmitted blue grey in the iris and the highlight on the eye, Phillip must have found a really
useful medium to help him achieve all this within the limitations of a demonstration portrait

15 Resin painting vehicles (c)

Section of white impasto with an even layer of glazed colour over the smooth surface

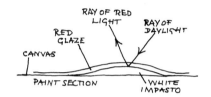

Section of white impasto with a graduated glaze which allows the white to emerge

Section showing white impasto painted roughly giving a pronounced brush stroke. The glaze runs into the grooves and can even rub off the projections

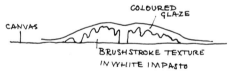

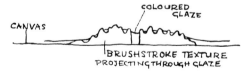

The technique of glazing is one that has a fascinating attraction for the student who has accumulated a fair amount of experience but is not yet fully at home in the painter's workshop. To use glazes of colour is both the simplest and yet the most difficult thing to do.

A glaze is no more and no less than the word indicates – a thin transparent layer of paint usually forming the final and finishing layer to a painting. It is simple because so long as a transparent pigment is selected, it can be mixed with a generous amount of medium and run over the surface of the painting. The work already done shows through and an added gleam of colour is achieved without the bother of having to attend to drawing and detail – that will show through the glaze. This sounds a rather attractive simplification, and quite a lot can be done with an intuitive manipulation of paint in this way. Where there is a strong conception of the subject, techniques are evolved as they are needed. That is how all techniques have been established. The analysis comes afterwards.

However, if all this is left to chance the student may find himself muddling around and the inspiration which should give life to his skill, leaks away in delays and frustrations.

Glazing is a time honoured painting practice evolved in the sixteenth century in the Venetian School and used widely in the seventeenth and eighteenth centuries and so it is as well if a painter of today undertakes a few exercises involving the processes of glazing so that when the need arises the means are ready to hand. Instant improvisation is unscholarly when such a wide vocabulary of means of expression have already been exemplified in the work of practised masters.

If the canvas is painted with solid impasto – where for instance a rich medium of stand or sun thickened oil with dammar varnish is used, this must be followed in the glaze by an appropriately increased richness in the glaze medium. If the paint for the glaze is simply diluted with a lot of turpentine to spread it, it will sink in, go mat, lack depth and even lose its transparency in a sort of mat bloom. All this happens if the law of painting 'fat over lean' has not been observed. The first thing to prepare in making a glaze is a vehicle a little richer than that used in the previous painting. Saturating the surface with linseed oil will not serve the purpose. It will take too long to dry and will not 'stay put' sufficiently. It is necessary to use a resin vehicle or one of the resin/oil blends.

Some pigments are by nature more transparent than others. To test them, a small amount of colour from the tube smeared on glass will show, which allows the light to penetrate when it is held up to the window.

Flake white, yellow ochre and venetian red are almost completely opaque and will let very little light pass through. Veridian green, on the other hand, allows a great deal of light to pass through; so also does rose madder, alizarin crimson, French ultramarine, cobalt blue, magenta and Indian yellow. These are the transparent colours and produce the stained glass window effect. All these pigments, crimson, other lakes and even such an earth colour as terre vert will transmit light most beautifully. Once mixed with the chosen resin vehicle they become more transparent and even the more solid pigments can acquire some of that quality. Burnt siena and burnt umber, though low in tone, will allow some light to penetrate the paint film. Many strong blues such as Prussian, monastrel and Winsor blue are very much influenced by the tone of the underpainting they pass over, showing their full blueness over a white ground but disappearing when they pass over a dark brown, into blackish obscurity. Used thinly with a glaze vehicle quite solid pigments such as cerulean blue, cadmium orange, cadmium red and vermilion can be brought in to play a part in glazing.

So far we have not considered what is happening to the picture that, at a rather crucial moment in its development, has the underpainting submitted to a treatment like

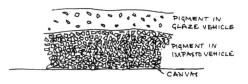

A very much magnified section of paint structure showing how the grains of pigment in the impasto, immersed in a stiff resin vehicle are isolated from the pigment grains suspended in the glaze medium. The lead white of the impasto has no contact with the vermilion of the glaze. No chemical interaction is possible but rays of light can pass unimpeded and reflect the white through the red. This was used in painting the head of the pheasant in the coloured illustration facing page 48

Alizarin crimson glaze in various degrees of strength were painted over black lines. These show through completely in the paler shades

that in the Christmas pantomime, when the coloured spotlights suffuse the good fairy in pink light and the demon king in deathly greens and lurid reds.

Glazing can be used spontaneously or it can be the final and enlivening stage in a deliberate and careful build-up as it was used in very many old master works now to be seen in our galleries.

This building up involves more than one stage of underpainting. One method is a smoothly modelled monochrome of white paint of varying thickness on a dark ground. The first illustration shows this stage. I painted this head from a cast of a nineteenth century sculpture using a canvas prepared in a way that we believe approximates to that described by de Mayerne as the method of Rubens. I mixed charcoal, ground to a powder, with egg yolk and painted it on the canvas with rough criss cross strokes. On this the flake white modelling was built up. The parts

Nineteenth-century sculptured head 16 in. × 12 in. – 40 cm × 30 cm oil painting by CATHERINE MOODY at the stage previous to glazing. The black ground was prepared with a coat of charcoal powder in egg yolk tempera medium. The free brush strokes are emphasised, then the modelling of the head is built up with flake white only, using it thickly in the full light, rubbing it in very thinly and smoothly with a finger tip in the half lights. This painting has been photographed at the white on black stage with no mixing of white *with* black

of the subject receiving light were loaded with white impasto; where the shadow encroached, the white was rubbed in thinly so that it only half obscured the dark ground and finally faded away completely until, for the shadow, only the black textured ground was showing. Consequently a good deal of ground is untouched. The solid appearance of the head is evoked by the selection of the part projecting into light. There is no mixing of the white with black; there is no grey in the painting; only the impression of half light arising from the thinning traces of white.

The next stage would be continued when the white is firm (not necessarily bone dry) by tinting with colour. Yellow, red, blue and green, either as pure colours or mixed to make appropriate tints, are gently laid over the white, very thinly, and gradually the colour is reached without alteration of the established light and shade.

Such a process was described in detail in an article by John McLellan with notes by the present author.[1] McLellan followed as faithfully as possible the description by de Mayerne, a friend of Rubens, of the method used by Rubens and Van Dyke.

The initial modelling in this method depends on the same varying thickness of the white on the grey ground. The glazing colour is added in separate layers of warm pigments. The white is laid on with a brush or a finger tip. The object being to keep the surface smooth. This is necessary because only with a smooth surface can you control the glaze. If you have a heavily textured white that dries with deep furrows you cannot prevent your glaze from running off the bumps and into the grooves. The colour therefore becomes intense in the furrows and slides off the projections leaving them almost white. This may be satisfactory in painting landscape or folds of drapery but if a portrait is being painted and the attempt is being made to suggest the peach bloom complexion of the cheek of a youthful model, then heavy brush texture in the underpainting will give the effect of wrinkles and a worn appearance.

Another variation of this method was practised by William Etty RA 1787–1849. When a student I made a full size copy from the original nude by Etty. As far as possible I

An academic copy of a Nude by WILLIAM ETTY. 18 in. × 25 in. – 45 cm × 62.5 cm. Copy painted by CATHERINE MOODY from the original in the Victoria and Albert Museum, London. This copy is unfinished, showing two preliminary stages. The initial brown monochrome shows in the right hand background; the build up of white alone can be seen in the right shoulder and arm. The development of colour and form in the rest of the nude is achieved by gradual and controlled addition of colour in glazes. The drapery on the left shows the vigorous brushwork of the white impasto covered with a simple glaze of veridian. This has been allowed to run into the channels of the impasto. The speedy painting of the drapery contrasts with the masterly control in Etty's original, of modelling and colour in the figure

[1] *Leisure Painter*, 'A traditional Method Revived' Moody and McLellan, May 1976.

recapitulated every stage of the picture's development. The original is in the Victoria and Albert Museum. My copy is reproduced here and as it is unfinished it shows in three layers, the three separate stages of work.

A development on the earlier method is the fact that Etty lays in the whole picture in a warm brown monochrome. This takes the place of the all over textured grey ground of the method of Ruben's period.

Etty created the whole form of the composition and the modelling of the nude with a thin mixture of some brown such as burnt umber and ample turpentine. This was painted on quickly and freely in the background and drapery; rather thinly and dryly in the modelling of the figure. The decisive lighting of the studio north light means that there is quite deep shadow on the right hand side of the figure which, passing through a gently graduated shadow, changes to fully illuminated light. This was done with a fairly dry brush which made the change from the deep shadow to the plain white of the priming of the board with no apparent texture of brush strokes. A little of this half tone can be seen on the right shoulderblade and deltoid muscle of the shoulder. A finger tip helped in achieving

a gentle graduation. No white was used until the next stage where, like the previous method, the lights were built up with solid white. Tube white contains too much oil and so the pigment was spread on some clean blotting paper for an hour so that the excess was sucked out. Then, with a palette knife it was scraped off the blotting paper, placed on the palette and mixed with a resin emulsion vehicle which facilitated the build up of the impasto and accelerated the drying. This was applied with a brush and a finger tip to rub a thinning film of white up to and into the thin brown monochrome half light. (As flake white contains lead, if you do this remember to wash your fingers clean immediately.)

When the smooth surfaced white was satisfactorily modelled and drawn, then the glaze began. When the white was firm, but not too dry I took three parts of dammar varnish, one part of sun thickened linseed oil and a variable amount of turpentine – about three parts – to make the glazing vehicle. I mixed rose madder and yellow ochre. This produced the delicate warmth and pinkness of the nude. Half lights brought a tincture of cobalt blue and reflected lights had yellow ochre and a little burnt siena to enliven the

Paint samples showing, *left*: roughly textured brushwork. *Right*: a smoothly modulated underpainting. The lower band is of alizarin crimson glaze painted evenly over both. The second band shows on the right how further modelling is achieved on the smooth surface by graduating the glaze. A development of this technique is used in the Etty nude. See also diagram page 62

warmth in the shadows where one leg receives a reflection of light from the other. The glaze was very thin in the lights, gathering strength of colour and consequently tone, away from the highest light and on the curves to the half lights and shadow.

In contrast to the smooth modelling of the figure's form, the drapery is done quite roughly. The flutes and folds were built up with the same flake white treatment but the rough brush marks were left. The result is that the green drapery – achieved by an unmixed glaze of veridian – has collected strong but bright colour in the furrows, and bright intense green on the ridges of the white. The glaze also goes over the shadow of the folds. Here the glaze changes completely and a deep receding green, like the depths of a weedy pool, suddenly appear. (The unfinished part on the lower right hand side shows the first umber lay-in of the shadows.) The texture is, within bounds, accidental but the calculated contrast and change of quality was, in the original entirely under Etty's control. The degree of change encompassed as the eye moves from the smooth, bright warm tints of the finely modelled back to the freedom, richness and depth of the painting of the drapery, give a wonderful vitality to the original. This unfinished copy shows the initial brown monochrome in the background and the right shoulder; the built up white in the right shoulder and arm; the final glazing of the back, buttocks and legs could have had more and richer colour brought in by degrees to more nearly approach the vital colour of Etty's original. I did not reach the full finish but by having an incomplete copy I have a record and analysis of each step I made in endeavouring to follow the procedure in Etty's most enlightening study.

Gareth Hawker, taking a course with me on Academic Portrait Painting in the summer at Malvern School of Art, followed a procedure very similar to that of William Etty. One difference was that in order to speed up the work so that the whole process could be condensed into the three day course, Hawker recommended to students the use of some modern equivalents to traditional media. Using acrylic white paint for the build up,

instead of the traditional flake white oil paint reduced drying time to ten minutes or less. Then for the glaze he recommended Winsor and Newton's *Liquin* with oil paint. This allowed a second glaze layer to be attempted on the second day – 'as long as the paint was applied with a deft touch', was Hawker's proviso. His comment on the use of acrylic paint was that if drawing was found to be faulty a glaze could be wiped off with rag and turps and the underpainting reassessed and repainted within a few minutes, an obvious advantage during the limited period of a short course. Except for this special need Hawker prefers the richness and variety of surface given by traditional oil painting which acrylic white paint cannot rival.

One last but perhaps most interesting use of the technique of glazing is its ability to isolate the pigment grain. Sometimes it is desirable to use, in mixing a colour, pigments that are not entirely happy together. One example is the combination of vermilion with flake white. In the list of even the best and purest of pigments the manufacturers will caution users against mixing these two colours.[2] They can act chemically against each other and the result will be that in time the colour blackens.

In painting a still life group with a pheasant I needed very bright red and blue colours. The fleshy appendage round the pheasant's eye and beak known as the wattle is, in the cock bird, of a really vivid hue. I painted the bird on a succession of gloomy winter days when shadow obscured those parts of the head away from the light, but the coloured wattle received the highest light. Vermilion was the one colour that had to be used for the red. I needed it in several tones. It is easy to darken vermilion. It is perfectly safe to mix it with black or brown but making it lighter presents two problems. One is the danger of chemical action between vermilion and flake white. The other is a problem of optical colour. If you add white to vermilion you do not get brighter vermilion, but you *do* get a pale and rather unpleasant blotting-paper pink. There was no pink about the pheasant, but there *was* a facet of brighter red. How could this be depicted without the dilution and distortion of the vermilion's pure colour? This is where the

---

[2] Excellent catalogues are produced by Artists' Colourmen particularly Winsor and Newton. The lists of colours, their composition and permanence and their information on solvents, media and varnishes should be learnt by heart; the information is simple, clear and essential to know.

The Pheasant oil
18 in. × 16½ in. −
45 cm × 41 cm by
CATHERINE MOODY. See
also colour plate

glaze solved the problem. I painted the wattle in solid white (from which the excess oil had been dried out and Maroger medium added to make it handle well). Then when this was nearly dry I took some copal oil medium and a very little turpentine and mixed it with pure vermilion. When I had a pleasant handling glaze mixture I slid it over the top of the white. The white shone through lighting up the red. This stained glass effect of transmitting the light completely avoided the blotting-paper pink effect. It gave the range of tone from darkened vermilion through pure vermilion to the highest light of brightened

vermilion. Into the bargain the grains of the two pigments, each surrounded by a coating of resinous medium, were isolated from each other and therefore there was no chemical interaction.

For the blue parts of the bird's wattle I did exactly the same thing with ultramarine. I mixed this heavy dark blue with the glaze medium and made a very thin film flow over the impasto of white. A flat sable brush is sometimes useful for this action as it is soft and smooth and does not disturb the underpainting. The white lit up the blue which by nature is very transparent. In the half light a thinner underpainting of white showed its full blue colour and over the dark underpainting the ultramarine looks almost black. Again the sequence of richly colourful tones enabled the shape to be modelled in a controlled way. There is no danger of chemical interaction between these latter pigments but the jewel like quality sought for could only be achieved thus. White *mixed* with ultramarine would produce quite a different effect.

The science of optical colour is another subject and its use is a valuable element in the painter's vocabulary. This one example shows that the employment of a glaze is a most useful means of using optical colour to the full.

In addition there are quite a few colours that are incompatible and can interact chemically in a disastrous way. It is worth developing the glazing technique because of its convenient capacity of isolating the warring pigments. By

The Iris oil 10 in. × 8 in. – 25 cm × 20 cm by CATHERINE MOODY. Purple and violet are the darkest colours of the spectrum. How, then can the brilliance of the Iris be conveyed when its richest colour tends to sink into obscurity and gloom? Here, where the dark flower has to compete with pale yellow greens and near white, the colour was sustained with a solid built up impasto of flake white. Before the impasto was dry but was stabilized by the addition of Maroger medium, the colour was gently laid over the white, using ultramarine blue, magenta and rose madder in the glazing vehicle of copal oil medium (and a little turps). With this the shape of the petal, its velvetiness and the range of colour and tone were explored

The Pugin Drawing-Room at Eastnor Castle oil 31 in. × 21 in. –
77·5 cm × 52·5 cm by CATHERINE MOODY. This interior of a Regency castle
was designed by Augustus Welby Pugin. It was completed in 1852, some
years after the castle was built. The Gothic Revival splendour having a
mysterious quality when the sunlight, filtered by creepers, reflects from the
floor to dimly illuminate the vaulting of the ceiling and the tapestried walls.
Although the canvas is fairly large, the need for precise detail meant that
much of it was painted thinly with very localised impasto for the colourful
and gilded passages
See also colour plate facing page 49

its employment the full range of colours can
be used. You are not inhibited from using any
but the narrow choice of entirely permanent
colours.

How colours are used counts for a great
deal. Sound experience can give freedom.
The French painter Francois Boucher,
1703–1770, managed to use blue bice, a
colour that normally is condemned for going
green in linseed oil – yet in his portrait of
Madam Pompadour in the Edinburgh National Gallery, his blue has remained clear,
delicate and beautiful to this day.

16 DRAWING

The pencil and other drawing instruments

I have considered the various painting vehicles, assuming that the reader has already begun to paint, so this book is not so much on 'how to do it' as to give something of the knowhow of an active working studio to one who is just feeling his or her feet. One does not learn to draw by reading about it. It must be practised so that the eye and hand are trained to work together on the exploration of shape that leads to the full understanding of form, mass and space.

To help the reader make the most use of his observations of the drawing tradition it may help to review the various tools of drawing. As with painting media it is needful to choose the tool that suits the worker or the job.

When making a study of the work done by the old masters a great deal can be learnt from their drawings as well as their paintings. Everyone who wishes to become proficient in painting needs to have a firm basis of drawing. Shape, proportion, perspective, light and shade are dealt with in drawing. The element of colour that paint can bring needs to go hand in hand with all the foregoing aspects.

Cennino Cennini writing his *Treatise on Painting* published in AD 1437 proscribes drawing as an initial need and speaks of its use in the interpretation of light and shade.

We have now an excellent range of pencils available. There are also a wealth of drawing instruments related to the pen: felt pens, fibre tips and ball points. These are easily obtained and their characteristic is the effortlessness with which they can be wielded. These do not need to be described because their potentialities can easily be found by trying them

out. It is simple to find which suits one's purpose best. A word of warning, however, is necessary. Some of these recently developed drawing instruments are far from colour fast. One may modestly maintain that one's work is not intended for posterity. On the other hand it can be too frustrating if one has made notes for a picture and, leaving the drawing on a board in the light, or inadvertently leaving a sketch book open, the result in a month or two is that the vigorous black line you began with has faded to a faint greenish and incomprehensible stain. The normal graphite pencil – although it can be removed with a rubber – is completely fast and reliable.

So also are the traditional inks – Indian ink and Chinese stick ink. The pens used in the past were made from reeds and quills. The strong primaries from the wing and the tail feathers of the turkey and goose are ideal for a drawing pen. The quills should be hardened by warming them in the ashes under the fire, taking care they do not scorch. Then the elegant plume is stripped off. The pen wants to be no more than 7 in. – 17·5 cm long. (Any plume on the quill should be left to fanciful historic representations on the stage.) With a sharp narrow pen-knife blade the tip should be pared to leave a generous half of the diameter for one and a half inches of its length. The two shoulders of the tip are then cut separately. The cleft is the most difficult part to do. A start can be made with the point of the pen-knife pressing on the centre of the point of the quill, but the cleft really must be made splitting the tip by pressing upwards sharply with a paint brush handle from the inside. The cleft needs to be only a $\frac{1}{4}$ in. – 6 mm long. Then it must be encouraged to close up by pressing the back of the pen gently on the

Rembrandt has left many memorable pen drawings. He would have used a quill pen. A well cut quill is very pleasant to use being more resilient than the metal nib. To cut a quill pen a very sharp, narrow bladed knife is necessary.

(a) About one third of the quill is pared off for about $1\frac{1}{4}$ in. – 3 cm parallel to its length, cutting both sides simultaneously.

(b) The tip is formed by two separate cuts each side, making two equal shoulders.

(c) The cleft in the tip is started with the point of the knife but its length is increased by placing a watercolour brush handle under the tip and raising it sharply. The split must then be closed by gentle pressure of the back of the pen on the paper.

(d) To form the point place the pen tip (top uppermost) on the domed lid of a bottle. (The domed curve allows room for the shoulder of the tip.) Hold the knife on the tip of the nib at a slight angle (to suit the angle the writer prefers), and slope the blade back so that it cuts a chisel edge. Then, without holding the pen, exert a firm, sharp pressure to sever the tip in one clean cut.

(e) The pen enlarged to show the required shape of the tip and the chisel edge which allows the sideways stroke to be the characteristic hairline of the quill pen.

(f) A narrow strip of springy metal shaped in an 'S' bend is slotted into the tube of the pen to make a reservoir. A blob of ink is put in at the tip with a watercolour brush

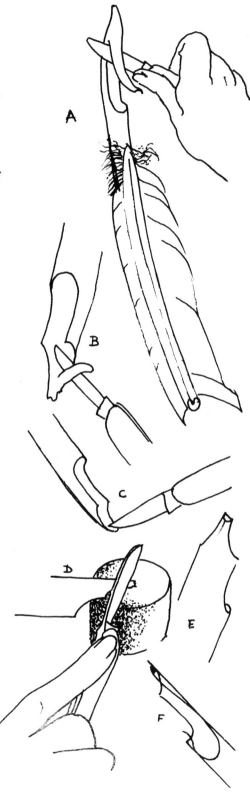

The Hat Shop by Henry Tonks 1862-1937
Reproduced by courtesy The Birmingham City Art Gallery
In spite of his disquiet about the art of his time, Tonks was producing such delightful work as this
composition. With a light but sure touch and delicate colour, this subject flowers very happily in its own
genealogical tree of tradition

paper. Lastly the tip is cut, slightly obliquely and to the right width for the work. It needs to be cut slightly obliquely to suit the angle at which the pen is held. It also needs to be cut with a chisel point so that the pen will give a fine hair line when moved sideways, a characteristic of traditional quill penmanship. This cut should be done by balancing the pen-top uppermost – on the convexity of a china saucer or bottle cap. Then, holding the pen by the tip with the blade of a very sharp knife, you press at the point at the required angle. A firm steady press and the pen springs free of the knife with a cleanly cut tip. Fit an 'S' shaped strip of springy metal for a reservoir and fill using a paint brush of freshly made Chinese stick ink. Equipped thus you have the tool of a Rembrandt.

The brown inks used in the past are a little difficult to identify. The sepia of the cuttle fish is a traditional medium and R T Cowern RA, tells me that some which he obtained from a Mediterranean fisherman proved delightful to use. Sepia is also useful as a wash and it was recommended for this by Varley the nineteenth century watercolourist. Pen and wash was a favourite combination for draughtsmen of the seventeenth and nineteenth centuries, Tiepolo, for instance, using it in a masterly fashion.

One of the earliest drawings in the collection of Christ Church College Picture Gallery, Oxford, is *An Archer of the Sienese School of the fourteenth century*. This is a brushpoint drawing on vellum. It is done so that it shows the distinct strokes of the hatching. It would be similar to the kind of treatment used in egg tempera underpainting and the medieval stained glass painting of heads and hands. It suggests that it was done by an artist used to illuminate on vellum in books. It is of that scale the drawing being about 6 in. – 15 cm high.

When speaking of 'drawing' as distinct from 'pen drawing' the pencil is the tool that comes most readily to mind. It is as well to realise that the pencil as we know it today is a comparatively recent development. Draughtsmen such as Leonardo da Vinci or Raphael would not have taken up a 4B as we know it now. A careful study of old master drawings will show that charcoal, red, brown and black chalk as well as pen and ink were frequently used. Tinted paper is familiar and on this the

value of white chalk is apparent. Holbein in the drawings in Windsor Castle often used red and black chalk for his portrait heads. Leonardo used lead point, Raphael used brown crude chalk, da Volterra used black Italian chalk, Van Dyke black and white chalk, Tintoretto black and white chalk on blue paper, and a Dutch master used a greasy crayon.

In a gallery of paintings the drawings have less impact than the paintings but it is worthwhile lingering for a time in this section. Often drawings show the work underlying the painting. It is also possible to find facsimile reproductions of drawings in book or folio form. With this a useful study can be made. One should first make sure that the facsimiles are full size and then if this is so, it is quite a good discipline to obtain the similar tinted paper and the nearest chalk or charcoal one can obtain and then make a copy of the work. As an aid to accuracy it is helpful to make a net of 1 or 2 in. – 2·5 or 5 cm squares on a transparent film which you can hold over the reproduction in the book. (A Royal Sovereign *Chinagraph* pencil will mark out the squares on the film.) You then divide your paper into a similar net of squares and mark out the main elements of the drawing section by section. This can be a most instructive study.

One speaks loosely of 'lead' pencil. Now pencils are made of graphite – a very pure form of carbon. This graphite, because of its molecular structure, runs particularly smoothly. Its molecules hold together in minute hexagonal plates. The electromagnetic attraction is all within the plane of the hexagons and there is little to hold the plates face to face and so they slide smoothly over one another. This is reflected in the smooth way the point of the pencil runs. It is an aid to drawing in that it enables the point to move quickly without dragging up the paper. It does not put one's teeth on edge as the chalk on the blackboard can, and as some 'carbon' (not graphite) pencils I have come across can also do.

England was probably the first country to use graphite. A deposit of natural graphite was discovered in Borrowdale in Cumberland in the second half of the sixteenth century. This was sawn into sheets and then divided into narrow 'leads' or 'slips'. This made an effective writing material which was then encased in cedar wood (*Juniperus Virginana*) the wood which cuts so cleanly to a nice, useful point, and smells so aromatic. Occasionally I have found old pencils with small square leads in the wood covering which suggests that they are the original Borrowdale graphite. They were quite expensive in the mid nineteenth century, with the net produce of the mine in six weeks working amounting to as much as £40,000.

Metallic points have been used from early times and the classic one of these is silver-point. It is necessary to prepare the paper with a coating that will enable the silver to get a 'bite'. Chinese white is a handy preparation and it is reasonably effective. The paper needs to be stretched as for watercolour painting and then a wash of Chinese white is laid over the whole area. When this is dry it will be found that on it a silver-point will make a delicate but firm line. The sketchbook of Villiard de Honnecourt, the Gothic draughtsman and architect shows the use of the silver-point on prepared vellum. With it he drew birds and beasts, all the crisp detail of the drapery of his figures and a number of technical diagrams.

This summer one of my students felt that silver point was a medium worth exploring. From the silversmithing department 2 in. – 5 cm of Standard silver wire was obtained; forged to a point and annealed to make it less springy. The hammering of the forging makes the silver hard, which is undesirable. By annealing it (ie heating it to a dull red with a blow torch) the silver is softened. By quenching it in the silversmith's acid bath it is made clean and free from impurity. If the facilities of a silversmithing room are not available the wire can be filed to a point and cleaned with Silvo silver polish. Fitted into a propelling pencil or an engineer's scribe the silver wire becomes a drawing instrument that is easily manipulated.

We made a ground from zinc oxide (the basic ingredient of Chinese white paint), tinted it with a little yellow ochre levigated powder colour and mixed it with glair. *Glair* is white of egg with water in the proportion of one of egg to three of water. This mixture is laid on in a wash on the previously stretched paper and improved by being ground on a marble slab with a marble muller or in a pestle and mortar. A fairly strong mark was obtained

on this with the silver wire and we found that it lent itself to crisp detail. The side of the point would produce a graduated tone. Some studies of plant form are the results of work and are here illustrated.

Our visitor to the school, R T Cowern RA, hearing of our explorations in this medium, has related his own recent experience of silver point.

Taking the precendent of the same Cennino Cennini mentioned earlier, he prepared a ground of calcined bone powder and size. He used a tablespoonful of rabbit skin glue – either level or slightly heaped – to one pint – half a litre of water. He toned this with the addition of a little levigated powder colour. With this he obtained a really rich mark, something between a 2B and a 4B pencil.

Cennini recommends that you collect the bones of poultry found where they had been thrown – under the dinner table! He recommends the legs and ribs of capons or old birds are the best. They should be burnt until they are whiter than ashes. Rather than go to these lengths it is possible to obtain from Wengers burnt bone which is an ingredient of bone china. This is used by Cowern. Occasionally he uses a little wax emulsion working from Max Doerner's recipe given in his book *The Materials of the Artist*.

Cowern recommends using a good hand-made paper for the base and notes that in time the silver line in the drawing becomes oxodized and develops a golden quality. He also observes that both creamy and pale grey grounds are pleasant to use. The grey grounds should be paler than the silver line but have just enough tone to allow the use of white chalk to heighten the lights.

By the early nineteenth century the pencil as we know it was beginning to emerge. John Thomas Smith, assistant to and biographer of Nollekins the sculptor, was writing in his *Book for a Rainy Day*, 'I walked home and found Isaac Solomon waiting to show me some of his improved black lead pencils.' This may have been a composition similar to the black lead used in the old days on the cast iron kitchen range.

The superb portrait drawings of the French painter Ingres seem to be executed in something similar to today's pencil and in Ingres' day the range must have been quite considerable. The Conté crayon – the square sticks of

hard, very slightly greasy chalk now obtainable in black, umber, red (sanguine) and white must surely have been invented by 'the ingenious M Conté' in the early part of the nineteenth century. When Napoleon invaded Egypt he was very conscious of its archaeological heritage. As well as an army of military men, he took an army of savants – historians, artists and draughtsmen – to record, catalogue and identify all their findings. With them was M Conté – on hand to manufacture

Plant Study 4½ in. × 3 in. – 11·5 cm × 7·5 cm. Silver point by Lynda Rogac. This was done on a prepared ground made of zinc oxide and egg white as a binder and tinted with a little yellow ochre. The silver point was a piece of Standard silver wire as used by silversmiths. The point gives fine detail and can be forged or filed to suit the draughtsman. Reproduced by courtesy of the artist

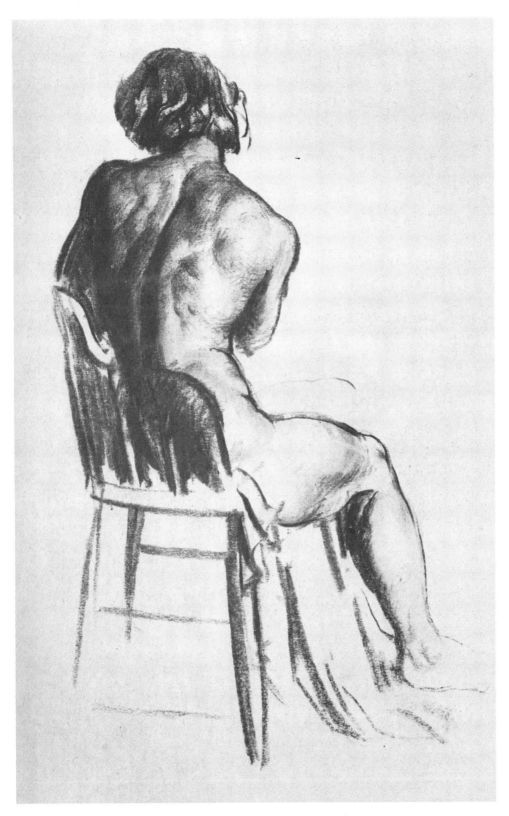

Nude Model Sitting
19 in. × 12½ in. –
47·5 cm × 31 cm
charcoal study by
VICTOR H MOODY

Right: *Jacob's Dream*
20¾ in. × 15¾ in. –
53 cm × 40 cm by
VICTOR H MOODY. This
compositional drawing
on the Biblical subject
was worked out as a
preliminary to painting.
He used charcoal to
evolve the main form
of the group, stump to
build up the modelling
and as the drawing is
on blue grey paper
further strength was
obtained by
heightening the lights
with a very pale cream
pastel

a great variety of instruments, drawing materials and apparatus for both artists and naturalists. The marvellous antiquities, the temples, the sculptures, the scenery and the people were engrossing subjects for the artists. These wonders had slept largely unknown to Europeans since Roman times and every discovery they made as they progressed up the Nile with Napoleon's advance, fired them with enthusiasm and drove them to drawing and recording more and more industriously. They were constantly using up their pencils and further consignments were incessantly demanded from M Conté whose

Right: *The Shady Pool* 20¾ in. × 15¾ in. – 53 cm × 40 cm by VICTOR H MOODY. Charcoal on creamy grey paper, heightened with pale cream pastel, the stump used in detailed passages. A pastoral scene that could become a painting. This is likely to be the same size as the drawing

Triton with Nymph 6½ in. × 7⅛ in. – 16·5 cm × 18 cm by VICTOR H MOODY. Compositional drawing in charcoal, pencil and white conté on blue grey paper. A traditional subject from Greek mythology treated in a Renaissance frame of mind. Drawing is the medium for study from a subject. It is also the ideal means of evolving imaginative design. A lifetime of study of the human figure and animals enables Moody to develop this grouping of sea creatures from his mental concept

manufactory was in Cairo. So urgent was their need that before supplies could reach them the artists had raided the army stores for lead. Before the lead could be turned into bullets they had made them into lead pencils.

Perhaps we now take the ordinary lead pencil too much for granted. It is a beautiful medium and in the hand of a genius it creates a work of continual delight.

'If you make a little mistake' Cennini said 'take a little crumb of the bread, rub it over the paper and efface whatever you please.' Nowadays we are equipped with erasers and putty rubbers but for Dame Laura Knight a lump of bread was the only accompaniment to the pencil for study. After a session on a portrait drawing both Dame Laura and the sitter were surrounded with crumbs. Breadcrumbs rubbed over a drawing will clean it up if it is overworked and the paper will remain unsullied and ready for re-drawing. The other

necessity is a sharp pen-knife so that the point can be kept keen for fine detail, and tapered so that it can be used on the side of the lead to build up an area of tone with broad graduated strokes. The pencil is very accommodating in that a drawing begun in charcoal can be continued in pencil which will refine and make precise the larger forms 'roughed-in' by the broader medium. Reproduced with this article are some compositional drawings by Victor H Moody which show the use of charcoal alone, charcoal with pencil, and charcoal with pencil on grey paper heightened with white Conté crayon.

For every user, pencil is one of the most obedient as well as the most helpful means of making a study, exploring form, digging into problems and for expressing your own interpretation of the world before you so that the work leaves you more fully informed, and more visually enriched than you were before.

Right: *Tram stop, Moss Side* 11⅝ in. × 7½ in. – 29·5 cm × 19 cm. Pen drawing by CATHERINE MOODY. This episode had to be put down in haste before the impression faded. A bottle of Indian ink and an ordinary steel pen were to hand. The shadows of night time meant that the pen had to work hard, hatching in all directions and a finger smudge was used to hasten the formation of the shadow of the bus driver on the background of hoardings, and perhaps the back of the pen was helpful in spreading black shadow where it curved into darkness

Trees in the Vale at Rowley
4 in. × 5½ in. – 14 cm. Quill pen drawing by VICTOR H MOODY. It is unusual to find a modern drawing made with a quill pen. This goose quill was cut in the way shown in figure 52 at the beginning of this chapter, and a rich sepia ink was used.

All works by Victor H Moody reproduced by courtesy of the artist

17 The easel

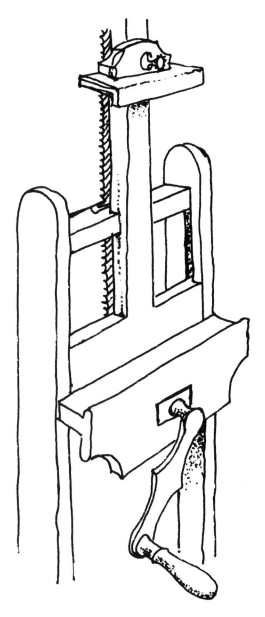

The nineteenth-century easel made of mahogany can be quite an elegant embellishment to the studio. Those with a vertical screw and handle whereby the picture can be wound higher or lower were specially desirable for the portrait painter

Left: *The Artist in his Studio* by REMBRANDT.
  Zoe Oliver Sherman Collection 38.1838. Reproduced by courtesy of The Museum of Fine Arts, Boston.
  This picture 10 in. × 12½ in. – 25 cm × 32 cm, shows the artist using a really substantial easel designed to support a large panel. It also gives a very characteristic rendering of the pose of a painter standing back and summing up his work. His painting hand is relaxed, holding his brush away from his clothes; the left hand holds the palette, a fair number of brushes and tucked in his little finger is a mahl stick used to support the painting hand. His wide brimmed hat shades his eyes; two extra palettes hang on the wall

An essential in the studio is a satisfactory easel. No study can be really peaceful if the student is interrupted by any shortcomings it may have. It is important that the canvas is held firmly so that the quick and vigorous dashes with a well loaded brush land exactly where intended. A faulty easel can do disastrous things. The legs can slip, the support of the canvas can descend or the whole thing can topple over – a traumatic happening for the preoccupied painter and possibly a black eye or other contusion for the model or for fellow painters.

In self-portraits of painters of two or three centuries ago an easel was a very simple affair but it was heavily built with massive timbers. Once set up it was very firm but it was meant to stay in one place. In the early days they were designed to support a heavy wood panel rather than the lighter canvas of more recent times.

Really the most reliable easel for studio use today is the Radial easel. It is firm but at the same time easily adjustable. If treated well it has a long life. Now it costs a lot of money but the making of an efficient easel is a skilled undertaking and the sound design of the Radial means that it is good value for money.

There used to be the occasional opportunity of acquiring an old easel from a well equipped amateur who was giving up a former pursuit. There is still a chance of finding one for those who enjoy such a quest. Country auction sales or sales in London studios, or even country junk shops are worth investigating. The design of nineteenth century easels was most diverse. Sometimes made of mahogany they can be an elegant embellishment to the studio now, as well as being very useful. Those with a vertical screw and a handle whereby the picture can be wound gradually lower or higher are specially desirable for the portrait painter. When at work it is very helpful to be able to wind the canvas down to do detailed work on the head, or make it rise when needing to work on the lower part of the canvas. With such a geared arrangement the painter can do this without any disturbance, even without relinquishing the palette, as only one hand is required to operate the movement.

However there is a note of nostalgia in this because these carefully made accessories, when discovered, are likely to be highly

priced, but an unhurried search can always bring the reward of patience. One dug out of the back of a shop might not compare too badly with a new easel.

The old-fashioned blackboard easel is not much use. The legs are so far apart that a substantial tray with a high back must be added to make sure that all but the largest canvas does not fall through. Then moving the picture up and down by replacing the pegs in their holes is a major operation. Improvising an easel is not to be recommended and even the most enthusiastic handyman will, when looking into the problem, usually find that it is not much use making do with half measures.

The painter, in the meantime whilst saving up, can make do with a rush bottomed chair. If the chair is opposite to the seated student a canvas will hitch quite safely on the corrugations of the rushes and lean against the ladder-back and a good deal of painting on a smallish scale and most drawing can be done in this way.

For landscape painters there is a good range of design and price of sketching easels. The chief thing is to make sure that the easel for out-of-doors is sturdy enough to hold a canvas in a certain amount of wind. Usually the spiked ends of the easel poke into the soft ground and make the base firm. It is worthwhile taking some stout string so that you can anchor everything by tying a lump of rock or a brick or whatever can be found handy and, by its weight, hold the easel down so that it will not take off in a breeze.

If the sketching easel is used indoors the spiked feet slide about on the polished floor and make holes in a carpet. A cardboard box with three or four books in it to weigh it down, provides a lodging place for the spike of the projecting back leg and the front ones can anchor on a strip of old matting.

It is necessary that the slides and screws of an easel are fully understood. Easels are always ready to play tricks on the unwary artist and unless the canvas is secure it cannot be relied upon to remain firm whilst the painting is in progress. A radial easel can

The painter, in the meantime, whilst saving up for a new easel, can make do with a rush bottomed chair

slope forward or back. When the painting is wet and inclined to glint or shine it becomes difficult to gauge the tone correctly. If the canvas is screwed on properly it is quite safe to pull the easel shaft forward and this reduces the shine. A foot placed on the base block and a firm tug at the top will usually bring the easel forward.

An easel is most helpful if the artist can be unconscious of it. There is a sort of love-hate relationship. Unless the painter approaches his easel in a determined way it will unleash a whole repertoire of practical jokes, the most common being the habit of dropping a wet and sticky canvas on the painter's forehead.

The Radial easel has three feet and the advantage of this is that whatever the unevenness of the floor, the feet are firm. An easel with four feet must have one that is adjustable. It is impossible to work on one that rocks to and fro. A large screw through one foot is the usual means of making it steady.

Very little maintenance is needed and nuts and washers should not be taken off except after many year's use when the sliding parts may get honed to a polish. If this happens the canvas tray may tend to slip even when the screw is tight. Then it is worth taking the tray and top holder apart from the shaft and sandpapering the moving parts, reassembling making sure that no butterfly nut or washer is mislaid.

It is a good idea to clean up the tray from time to time. Too much dry paint can build up and get in the way or dirty the brush when painting down to the bottom edge. To clean this it is best to use a paint stripper or solvent. One needs to be careful not to hack the wood and a stripper will soften old paint so that too much force does not have to be used to get it off. Paint stripper is harmless on an easel but it should not be used to clean a palette in case some traces remain to contaminate the new paint put out for use.

A Radial easel is obtainable from the leading artists' colourmen and it is an important invesment for anyone who intends to do a fair amount of work in the studio.

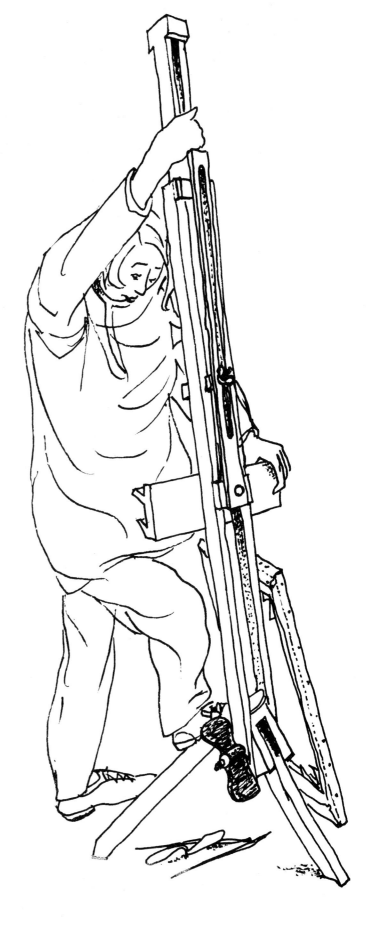

Between the painter and his easel there is a sort of love–hate relationship

The easel

Not all painters are interested in antique collecting but most have a feeling for craftsmanship. This Regency portfolio stand is a very handy piece of furniture to have in the studio. It provides the best means of storing and displaying drawings and prints. It is beautifully constructed and the mahogany is of fine colour

Another accessory of the studio is the lay figure. Miniature figures are of very little use but the full size figure is valuable both for the painting of clothes – the garments of a sitter who can only spare time for sittings for the head in a full or half length portrait. The lay-figure is also a very pleasant subject in its own right. Here *The Lay-Figure in the Costume of Flora*, oil 16 in. × 20 in. – 40 cm × 50 cm by VICTOR H MOODY shows that, although she had a finger missing, this figure could hold the draperies of the skirt with elegance. To make a studied analysis of drapery is an engrossing pursuit and such a figure enlarges the painter's scope tremendously. Full size figures made of papier-mâché in the nineteenth century are not easy to come by

18 BRUSHES

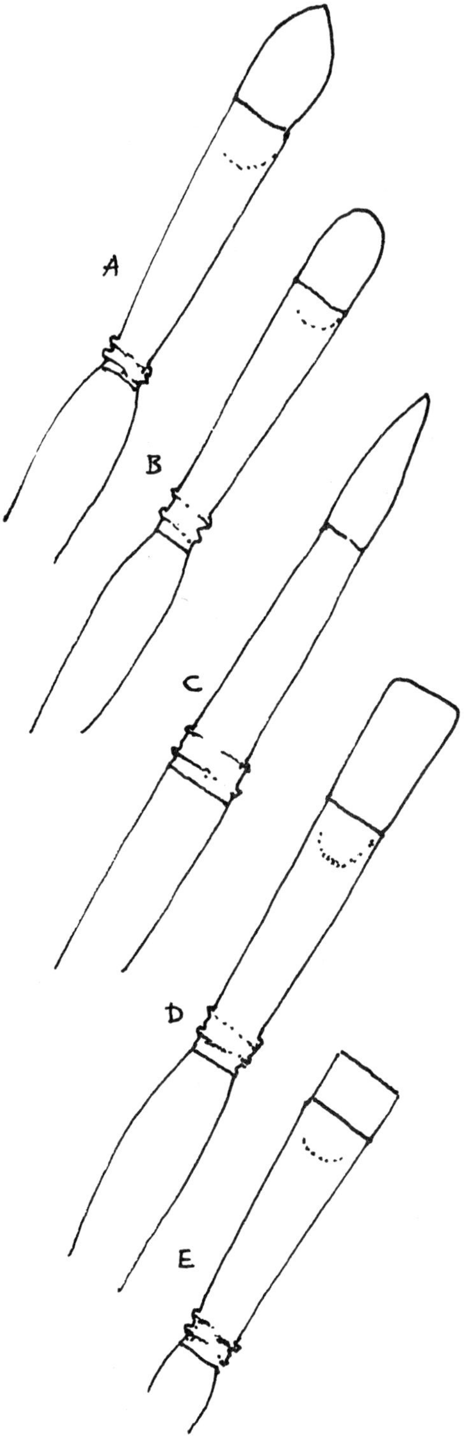

Many of the tools and colours used by the artist bear the names of former masters. In a few cases this is because the artists' supplier, when he has developed what he feels to be a good thing, adopts the name of a famous artist in order to popularise a new line. In most cases it is for the far more interesting reason that artists of standing have asked the colourman or brush-maker to make something which suits their particular needs. Consequently some of the usage of the painter's workshop is built into our everyday shopping for materials. None more so than the shape and character of paint brushes.

Hubert von Herkomer who had a school at Bushey must have had a very individual and controlled way of painting to demand those short bristled, thin, square edged brushes which bear his name. The firm of Robersons have a small history of art in their catalogue. There is an Orpen hog hair brush – as originally supplied *exclusively* to Sir William Orpen. It is a nice filbert with middle length bristles. There is the Lucy Kemp-Welch Dark Ox, originally made for that artist who specialised in painting horses. It is an unusual brush for oil painting – a short dome shaped point made of soft black ox hairs. There is the Leighton brush, a dome pointed brush made for Lord Leighton PRA in extra fine hog bristle. It just gives that extra insight to be able to look

Shapes of hog hair brushes;
A The filbert
B Domed shape – The Leighton
C The round which should taper to a point
D The flat; this can be in various lengths, but is best if it is not over long
E The thin short flat brush of the Herkomer type

A   B   C   D   E

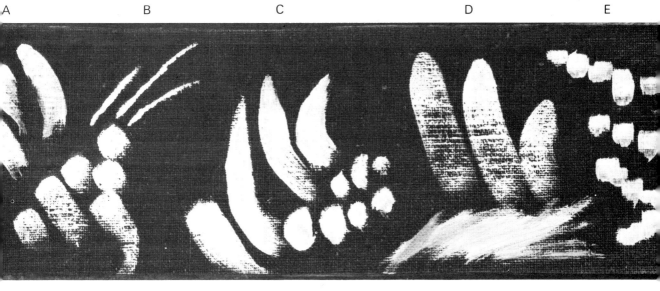

at the works of these painters and find in their painting evidences of the effect of the use of these particular brushes.

In oil painting, hog bristle brushes are the most commonly used. This white bristle is stiff and springy and whatever the consistency of the paint, a well made hog is strong enough to deliver it on to the canvas in whatever way the painter wishes. Oil painting brushes have long handles so that the painter can work at a reasonable distance from the canvas. Some painters like to use sable brushes. They are the normal thing for watercolour painters who use them with a handle length of 7 or 8 in – 17.5 cm or 20 cm. An oil painter using sables needs to find the ones designed for oil painting with long handles. This means that work can be done from the same distance as is usual with hog brushes. It is also important to use brushes of all the same length for another reason. One short brush held amongst the handful in the left hand can anoint all the other brushes with wet oil paint. This means the right hand gets filled with wet paint at every move.

Of the hog hair brushes a flat square ended brush with the bristles about as long as twice the width, is probably the one most commonly used. The hog bristles need to be as springy as possible and to have their naturally tapering points all trained inwards so that a compact tip is retained at all times.

I now use Rowney's series 120 flat hog and

Samples of brush strokes on canvas.
Distinctive strokes made by various brushes. Oil on canvas. *Left to right*:
A The Leighton
B Rowney 120 a flat brush that is very good for building up an impasto. Its chisel point is also good for building lines and edges
C Rowney 111 a round which is good with a flowing medium
D The Filbert carries paint well and also encourages sideways scrubbing and drawing with the brush
E The Herkomer, very short, square and thin, carries little paint and encourages a mosaic of touches of paint

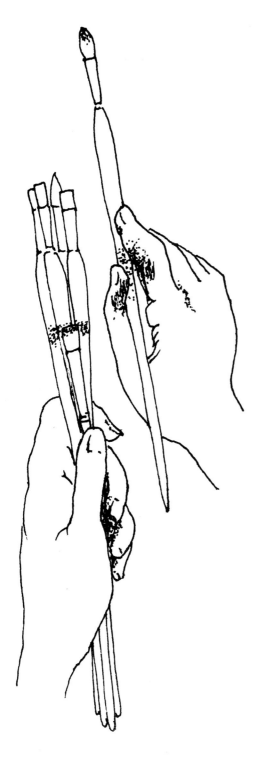

find these most satisfactory. The resilient hog bristles are nearly twice as long as the width. Flats are also made with shorter bristle – length about equal to width – and these are quite pleasant to use. A short brush means full control of the tip. When I began to paint I used the shortest of all, the Herkomer, which encouraged one to build up the work with a mosaic-like series of touches, but quite soon I took to using a longer haired brush which gives more freedom and play. I then sought a more expressive brushstroke. When choosing a brush it is wise to avoid any that appear *over* long. Too much length and the painter has hardly any control over the brush. The brush has to be flooded with medium to get paint to the tip and the ferrule is the only part of the brush that will follow one's movement. The better the quality of the hog bristle, the longer the brush can be. Spring and resilience make for full control over greater length.

Round brushes do not seem to be used as much as flats but with a flowing medium they work very well. I like to have one round brush (a Rowney series No.111) to three flats in my hand when painting.

The filbert is a time honoured shape. It is flat in the ferrule and shaped to a point at the tip. The filbert seems to encourage sideways scrubbing and the use of the brush as a drawing implement. It is pleasant to use in the early or monochrome stages of a painting where the drawing is being explored. Filberts can be had with short or long bristles and the Orpen filbert mentioned earlier seems to be just the right length.

Some painters like to lay their painting in with an outline and for this a sable is often used. A round or flat with long hairs is the tool for this. A long haired sable listed in some catalogues is a 'rigger' and an even longer one is the 'liner' or 'striper'. These are not often used – the 'rigger' belongs to the days when the painting of ships involved painting the fine lines of rigging, the ropes and spars; a specialised skill is needed to wield these brushes.

No brush is of any use that has its hairs cut off at the tip. I have tried to use a brush that had been cut and it tended to wipe the paint off the canvas rather than lay it on.

A good brush must be well looked after. It must be carefully cleaned and carefully dried. Brushes should be washed in warm water

One short brush held amongst the handful in the left hand can anoint all the other brushes with wet paint just at the point where they are held when painting. This means that the right hand gets filled with wet paint at every move

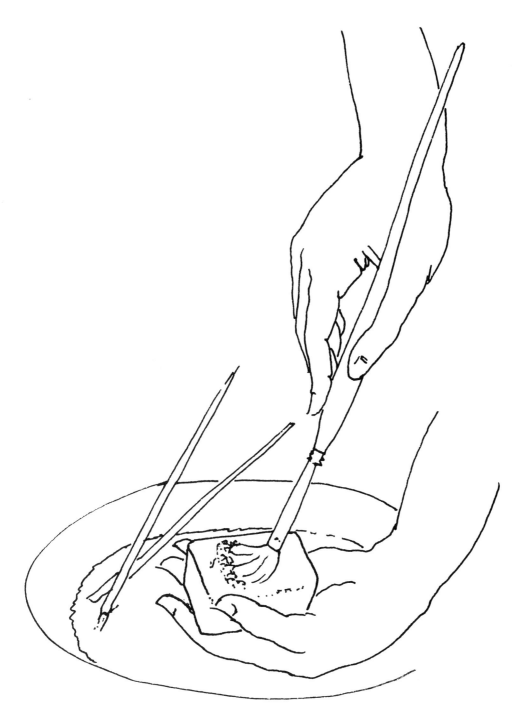

squeezing the ferrule down on a bar of soap and then gently pressing the soapy bristles into the palm of the hand, always stroking the way of the hairs. This must be done two, three or four times until every trace of colour comes out of the root of the brush. If there is to be a

Brushes should be washed in warm water squeezing the ferrule down on a bar of soap and then gently pressing the soapy bristles into the palm of the hand so that all traces of paint are cleared from the base of the brush

delay before washing the brushes they should have a preliminary rinse in turpentine. Indeed if painting is to continue on the next day a wash out with turps substitute or white spirit is satisfactory if a final rinse is made in clean genuine turpentine, to remove the last traces of colour. If varnish or a resin based medium has been used, only turpentine will be effective and the brush needs a turpentine rinse before washing in water.

When the brush has been washed it needs to be dried carefully. The bristles must be shaped up and held in place by cotton wound round the point or a long narrow strip of newspaper torn from the edge of the page, damped and rolled spirally round the bristle. The paper, in drying, will shrink and hold the point very tidily. A flat brush can dry very well on the mantelpiece with the foot of a pot or jar just resting on the tip. Wet brushes must not be put away in an airtight container.

Brushes of synthetic bristle, chiefly nylon, are used. They are, in handling, a cross between the hog and the sable brush. Nylon will not take the place of the natural materials but if the painter becomes used to handling nylon brushes they will be an additional element.

The brush is not the only instrument for painting. The palette knife can do the whole thing and produce a very lively and brilliant effect. The trowel shaped knife is most manoeuvrable. Robersons have a wide variety of sizes and shapes in their catalogue and Rowneys are particularly careful about the spring in the metal of the blade. For palette cleaning the spatula shaped knife is best and it is useful for laying-in a preliminary spread of paint for a sky or any large area that needs to be painted quickly and for mixing paint with the solid or buttery media on the palette.

It is also useful to have an ivory or a plastic palette knife. Egg tempera should not be mixed with a metal tool and there are one or two jobs such as preparing priming for canvas or a ground for silver-point or tempera for which a non-metallic knife is preferable.

As well as putting paint on it is sometimes necessary to take it off. Cuttle-fish bone is a very gentle abrasive and it is the traditional material for rubbing down dry paint when preparing to re-paint, as already described in chapter 10. It will remove over dominant brush strokes and also remove any

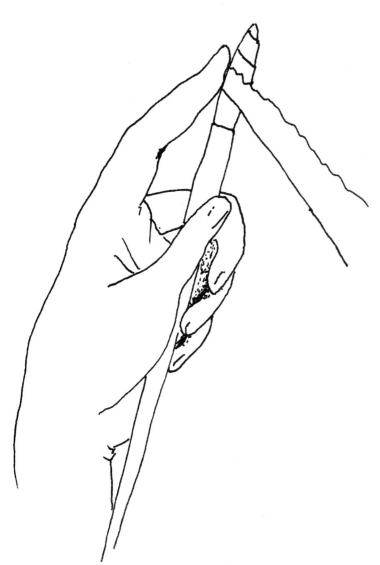

When the brush has been washed it must be shaped up and the bristles held in place. A long strip of newspaper damped and rolled spirally round the point will shrink when drying and hold the point very tidily

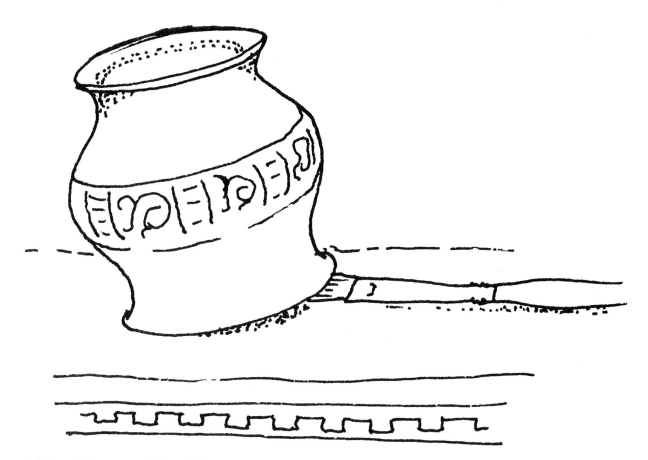

A flat brush dries to a good shape if the tip is put under the foot of a pot on the mantlepiece – preferably a heavy hand made pot and not a valuable one, in case of accidents

excessive coating of linseed oil which may have risen to the paint surface. A rub with the porous side of the cuttlefish will make the surface more receptive to further painting. Cuttlefish bone is found on the beach after a storm at sea. It is the silicaceous skeleton that develops inside the body of the many tentacled cuttlefish. It remains after the soft parts have rotted away and has a hard smooth crust which should be broken away round the edges and a crumbly, porous, abrasive inner mass which is the one to use. It leaves white powder on the dry paint which can easily be dusted off before painting is re-commenced. It is easily obtainable from pet shops, as it is sold for cage birds.

Another thing to keep in the paint box is a pointed pen knife. This can be used to scrape off any detail of the painting that needs improvement. It is also essential to have some point to prize off and penetrate the mass of dry paint that seals up an open tube that has lost its screw top. If the cap of a tube is fixed on solidly by dry paint, it damages the tube if force is used to twist it off. A lighted match held under the cap for a few moments will soften the dry paint. Holding the hot cap with a paint rag, a gentle turn will bring it off quite easily.

On a sketching expedition it is wise to have a box of matches or a cigarette lighter handy so that the painter, out in the country far from studio resources, is not denied access to tubes that have not recently been opened.

19 The studio

It is rare now for anyone to build a studio. The palatial house with studios built by Lord Leighton in Holland Park, London, is now used as a gallery. Leighton House is probably the most exotic of the many studios built by successful painters and sculptors in the late nineteenth century. Richly decorated, their interiors formed a background in keeping with the artist's way of life. The astonishing affluence of the successful painter in the 1880s to the 1890s is shown by the substantial houses and sumptuous studios of Holland Park and Melbury Road. Luke Fildes, painter of the memorable narrative picture *The Doctor* engaged the architect Norman Shaw to design his house. King Edward VII, whose portrait Fildes painted, said of his studio that it was one of the finest rooms in London.

In succeeding decades artists of more modest aspirations have been catered for by builders who erected rows of studios in the appropriate districts or 'artists quarters'. These were equipped with large, well lit studios with plenty of space and light but with simple, not to say sketchy living accommodation, an emphasis fully in accord with the artists' outlook. Sometimes the entrance to the group of studios was embellished with wrought iron gates and Italianate roof tiles encouraging a romantic atmosphere and the right attitude of mind in the visitor who was perhaps a prospective patron.

Today, studio building on the grand scale is really extinct but even the painter working quite modestly finds that there comes a time when canvasses overflow from the spaces in the sitting room or the spare bedroom. Many people who have taken up painting come to a point when they feel they must find some place specially suited to their activities. Many

are converting part of their houses or outbuildings.

Greenhouses, garages and tool houses that can be erected by the handyman are easy to come by. I have not yet seen a studio offered on the 'build it yourself' principle and until that comes it is necessary for the artist to make his or her own modifications.

It is best to know what to aim for before setting out on any undertaking. Simple adaptations are possible. A survey of the large purpose built studio of the past will demonstrate the main factors involved. From this each artist can extract what is necessary and what can be done to suit his particular needs.

A top light can sometimes be made by having some glass tiles inserted in a roof. This should be done on the northern slope. A garage can sometimes be floored in at halfway and the studio made in the roof space.

Older buildings often have an outbuilding such as a wash house which is no longer of use. Here a tall window could be made in the gable end of the building. It can be quite narrow but if it goes high up into the gable it will shed light into the far corners of the room.

A greenhouse produces too much light from all directions. Painting would go on more happily if screens of black polythene were fixed to the south side of the roof on the inside. A wooden tool-house might be made light enough by having some transparent plastic material used instead of roofing felt on the northern slope of the roof. The tilt of the ground or the existing plan of the garden may mean that the building cannot be placed with a north light. The nearest thing to the north, north east or north west will have to do and really does very well.

This kind of building is usually only habitable in good weather because of the difficulties of heating although anyone practising a craft and needing somewhere to do a job with clay or plaster can sometimes put up with rather rigorous conditions just for the time needed for making a cast. The job is so hectic in any case, that the activity keeps the craftsman warm. The work, on the other hand, must be kept free from frost as freezing completely destroys a clay model.

In any building a high window can be a great help in improving the lighting. The width in the opening is by no means as helpful. A narrow opening is structurally more stable. It does not require, at the top, a wide loadbearing construction. Structural stability must be considered with any modification and it should be remembered that planning permission may be needed before any changes are made.

Before planning any sort of studio it is worth looking at the classic studio design. Where a studio is to be used for portrait painting, for study from the model or for still life, the needs are specific. A clear steady light which will reach to the back wall of a room is needed. This allows a good light to fall on the model and still affords the artist plenty of room for canvas and easel in front of the model. The painter also needs to be able to walk back from his canvas so it is a disadvantage if everything has to be crowded up close to the window.

Today the classic studio lighting is hardly recognised. The north light which was *de rigueur* in the nineteenth century has been forgotten and its usefulness is not generally realised. For the new building for colleges of art, the architectural design of a studio has become rather generalised in its intention. In many places the life class has been jettisoned and the studio as the work place for the evolution of abstraction, constructivism or tachism has not crystallised as these ever changing movements pass or are replaced by others.

The north light and a high source of light was at one time synonymous with studio lighting and so universal was the need for it in the art world that a roof-scape in any region where artists congregated such as Chelsea or Fulham would present a vista of complicated dormers, roof lights and sky-lights together

(*Overleaf*) *The Studio of John Ward RA at Bilting* Pen drawing 18 in. × 12$\frac{1}{2}$ in. – 46 cm × 32 cm by JOHN WARD RA.

John Ward's work has the quality of always having been seen with a fresh eye and to the spectator his productions are ever felicitous in their artistry. Yet his work is more profound and, at the same time, more wide ranging than a superficial appraisal would reveal.

His Royal portraits are but a part of a numerous and varied output where each work is not only a likeness but also a picture that makes the sitter memorable.

Known to a great number of people by his illustration, his intellectual grasp of his subject matter in illustration and in his sketchbooks means that he is acquiring an ever growing visual vocabulary.

Now his outstanding works of portrait composition are on a grand scale. Problems of organizing on many strata both aesthetic and intellectual, means that his vocabulary of draughtsmanship and technique, have to equal the tasks he sets for his practised skill. All this being accomplished with 'the art that conceals art'. This glimpse into the studio, Bilting, gives an insight into the workplace of creativity.

The raftered roof of the converted barn, the lay-figure, the heaps of books, the casts all go towards evoking the studio atmosphere. Then the artist himself at work, with the light from the window falling on a vast canvas – his initial design resting on his knee, his right hand supported by a mhal stick – the first key points are being located and the spectator, whose eye passes down the length of the studio, past the *objets d'art*, the pots, bottles and lamps, comes to rest where. on the clean expanse of canvas, the artist is evoking the very magic of the studio.

Reproduced by courtesy of the artist

The Studio
at Belding
Mr Ward

An out-building can be made into an excellent studio by putting a tall window in the end wall and taking it up to the gable. This will fill the space with light much more effectively than a wide 'picture window'. It is also structurally satisfactory as it leaves plenty of support for the roof

with difficult areas of slating, valley gutters and the like where roofs had been thrust up and distorted to catch the essential north light. Top bedrooms had at one time blossomed into studios by this means.

Like so many things in painting, changes are linked with fashion and fashion arises from the deeper changes and phases in the approach to art.

For many decades now the phrase 'light and shade' has been ignored. Only in the last days of the 1970s has light and shade returned as a subject that can be given serious consideration. Students are returning to the study of the life model. Shadow which has been equated with dirt and muddy colour has again been recognised as the fundamental means for the understanding of shape and can be used to express the inner contours of solid form.

A source of clear and steady light is of the greatest value for study. When painting out of doors, sunlight and shadow is a delight, but whilst making the study of a head it is disconcerting to have a shaft of sunlight gradually pass with the hours across the subject – diversified by shadows from glazing bars.

An unchanging light is therefore the most satisfactory. The source of light from the north is the whole area of sky. It takes up the upper half of the view from the window and so the window needs to go up as far as possible. The light will then reach the far side of the room and reflect wonderful variations of colour and luminosity.

Nineteenth century schools of art derived great advantage from the tendency of the architects to build in the revived Gothic style with steep pitched roofs and high pointed gables. This allowed life studios to have tall pointed windows which were ideal for their needs. In the life class illustrated it can be seen how well the model is lighted and how quite a crush of students are accommodated in front of the model. See *An Edwardian Studio* page 102.

The Sunday or spare time painter may have to improvise but with the right sort of lighting in mind it may not be difficult to find a useful workplace. The infants' schools of the Victorian era now disused, retired railway stations and noncomformist chapels are again to be found full of activity where a group with

Wide window from interior

Section of room and light rays

(a) A wide window looks fine on a plan but the low letter-box mouth only illuminates a patch on the floor.
(b) A model sitting on a chair has only his feet in direct light as can be seen in the section of the room

work in mind are getting together. Stable and loft take on a new purpose when a model is found and a group gather together and gain mutual encouragement to further the study of the mysteries of art.

We began with the palette balanced on the thumb wondering what to put in the dipper. We end pacing out the studio. There are many subjects that have been touched upon, many jobs that need to be done have not been described. 'How to paint' needs to run into very many volumes but 'how to set about painting' is a different matter. With the right approach the student of painting does not need so much telling. In the right atmosphere of the studio it only needs a hint to set one on one's way and a glance at one's neighbour's palette is more useful than volumes of explanation. The studio practice of the fourteenth and fifteenth centuries was described by Cennino Cennini and most of his words are still appropriate. Many people derived much benefit from the teaching of J M W Turner – even if he did make a habit of leaving his notes for his perspective lectures in the cab! Richard Redgrave recorded that a problem he had with the dress of the figure in his Royal Academy exhibit was discussed by several Academicians. They thought the neckline was too low, the dress was shockingly décolleté. It was not until Turner stood before the canvas that the problem was solved and that by a nod towards the dress and a nudge with the two words – Too bright. It was too sharp a contrast that was disturbing and Turner went to the heart of the matter with two words.[1]

All that I have written has led me back to the fact that the work has its own momentum. If the painter is content to join the age old tradition of the studio then he will find the means of full expression. It is there and so long as he is at work so will it be discovered.

[1] *Richard Redgrave CB, RA*, F M Redgrave, Cassell, London, 1891.

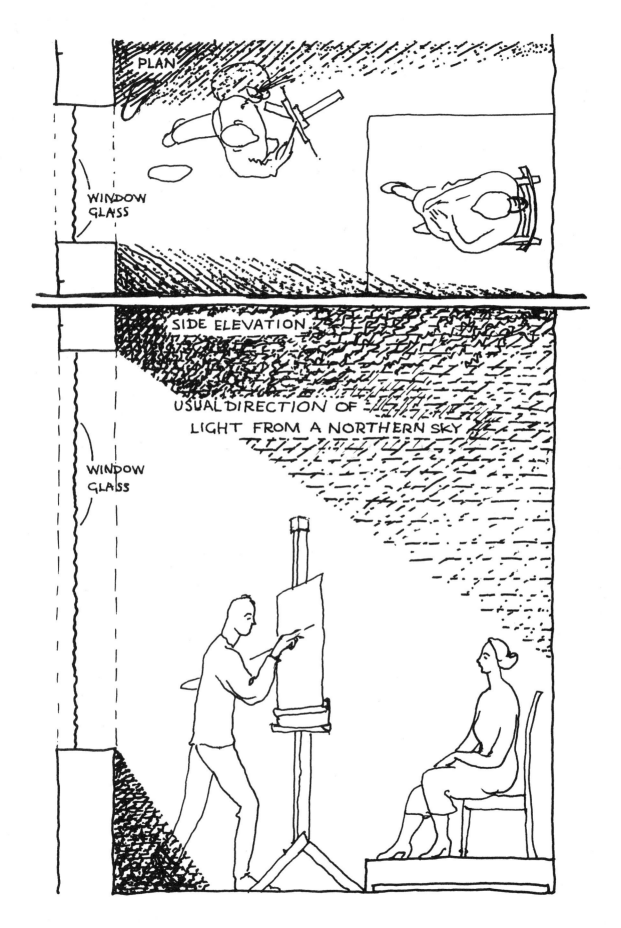

PLAN

WINDOW
GLASS

SIDE ELEVATION

USUAL DIRECTION OF
LIGHT FROM A NORTHERN SKY

WINDOW
GLASS

Rossetti Studio, Flood Street Chelsea. This was, at one time, the studio of Norman Hepple RA. Before that it was used by Augustus John and William Orpen who ran a school of art there. Before that it was the studio of Dante Gabriel Rossetti and so, situated in Chelsea, traditionally London's artists' quarter, this studio is full of painterly atmosphere. The column and the staircase are there for the backgrounds of portraits in the grand manner. In this photograph it must be summer because Hepple is leaning against a fine example of the time honoured 'Tortoise Stove' which for many decades has warmed the fairly spartan models.
  Photograph lent by Norman Hepple RA.

Left: (a) The plan and section of a studio with a tall narrow window. This window will allow light to fall right across the room and on to the back wall.
(b) The model's head is in direct light. There is plenty of room to have the model well back, allowing the painter to stand between the model and the window. There is also room for him to walk back and review his work. Daylight from the north, reflected from the sky and clouds enters the window at about 45 degrees

A student's studio. Everyone who paints likes to have some sort of refuge to work in. Often I have joined in planning how rooms can be converted or studios improvised as soon as the painting fever is caught by a student. Mrs Theodas describes hers as, 'A small hut at the bottom of the garden, about 14 ft × 6 ft – 4.2 m × 1.8 m, with no north window or top light at all – but I love it dearly in spite of no space and continual clutter.' And she continues, 'At least people can see that lack of space does not deter one!'

Left: *An Edwardian studio*. As the lady students' dresses and hairstyles indicate, this was photographed about 1910. It shows by the glint of light on the cross-bar, the height of the window. The beams of the roof structure show that it is a building in the nineteenth century Gothic Revival style and therefore is likely to have tall pointed windows. The whole of the model is illuminated and light reaches even into the corners round the base of the cast of the Classical marble of *Jason* in the foreground. The model is placed well back in the room so that there is a space for over a dozen painters to work from her. The casts which include Michelangelo's *Tondo* and the *Slave*, *The Clapping Faun* and *Discobolos*, give an atmosphere of study and scholarship

Left: *Norman Hepple's studio window*. Drawing by NORMAN HEPPLE RA. This drawing of Norman Hepple's studio shows all the elements needed in the ideal workplace. Painter of many Royal portraits, Hepple takes a leading place today in the classic tradition of formal portraiture. His comprehension of space and atmosphere in his paintings is based upon a firm grasp of perspective interpreted in terms of accurate tonal relationship. This means that he has a trained and unerring eye. The sure foundation of structural drawing means that Hepple, in painting either a single portrait or grouped figures, has a great command of form and composition. His numerous pictures of interiors where figures move naturally and felicitously are so well harmonized that to a spectator, a complete understanding of all the richness of the conception is accomplished with no consciousness of the interposition of the painter's technique. He achieves a full expression of reality. He values the academic approach and remembers the specification for a studio light – four feet square and nine feet from the ground – given by Sir Joshua Reynolds, the Father of the Royal Academy and the academic tradition.

In the diagrammatic detail of this drawing can be seen the six blinds that give an almost endless permutation of positions and sizes for the light source. Three of the blinds work from the top and three from the base. For the work in progress all three of the lower and the left hand top window sections are covered leaving a square of illumination from the other two sections. In addition to this the studio has plenty of cupboards and a sink to hand for washing brushes. For the sitter in winter who may be a lady wearing evening dress or for the nude model, there is a huge bank of radiators under the window and at the far end of the room, to provide warmth.

Then the painter and his easel is shown in a position where he can see the model fully illuminated and where he has room to move back to review both his canvas and the sitter. The high source of light allows his canvas to be brought within the zone of shadow under the window so that it is not glaringly bright. This helps in assessing correctly the tonal relationships.

Reproduced by courtesy of the artist

Mrs Boswell's studio. An area of glass tiles built into the roof as in this studio is a great help to the light within. This building has wide windows and a useful long panel in the doors

Interior of the same studio showing how the patch of glass tiles greatly extends the volume of illuminated space, allowing pictures hung high on the wall to be seen

Right: *Studio windows put into a Victorian house.* A chimney built into this gable of a house of 1870 might seem to preclude the addition of a studio light, but the chimney strengthens the wall and two narrow windows have been made that provide a good north-east light. The windows were carried up through the ceiling of the room into the roof space, adding another, very useful two feet of height

A garage loft. Glass tiles laid in the roof of a student's garage has made the loft space into a useful studio

Work in progress in the same studio. A view taken from under one of the tall narrow windows showing how far the light penetrates into the room. There is plenty of room for the painter, Victor Moody and his canvas. The sitter, Lt Commander Holmes is in a clear even light and placed well back in the room

Right: *The Great Studio, Leighton House.* First built in 1866 by Lord Leighton, President of the Royal Academy, it is probably the most exotic of the many studios of the great and famous of the late nineteenth century. Leighton built his house to meet his personal and working needs. These were on a grand scale. The interior is rich with decoration. Classical and oriental features required the use of marbles and ceramics, columns and arches, coffered and domed ceilings are all an extension of his artistic creativity. This exterior shows the size and height of his studio window which provided light for a room of 25 ft × 60 ft with a height of 17 ft – 7·6 m × 18·2 m × 5·1 m. In this building the amplitude and importance of the conception of painting is epitomized. This did much to establish the standing of the visual arts in that period, a conception which holds to this day.
Reproduced by courtesy of the Royal Borough of Kensington and Chelsea

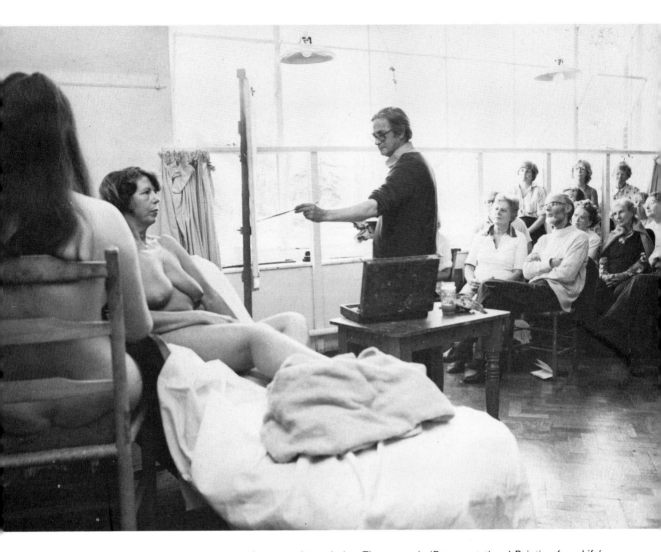

Bernard Dunstan RA *demonstrating painting*. The course in 'Representational Painting from Life' established by V H Moody, Principal, at Malvern School of Art in 1961 has brought a number of students together in succeeding years to see a master painter at work. Here Bernard Dunstan RA is working in the main studio making use of an oblique lighting from the large north window. Not quite as tall as it should be, this window, nevertheless, provides ample light for a large number of students to work from the model.

Reproduced by courtesy of the artist

Bernard Dunstan RA, the models and his painting in progress. Working on this composition of two models in 1979, Dunstan showed a rare talent for immersing himself in the work in hand and allowing the numerous audience of students to watch the painting grow. The painting was by no means a routine demonstration done to a formula, but a true work of art in which the elusive qualities of the situation are distilled with delicacy and sensitivity, whilst the foundational structure was also fully apprehended. The simple requirements of the traditional studio, fulfilled in this building, enabled students to take up their brushes, following the demonstration and soon find their way in their individual quest in study from the model. In this photograph the model to the right has her back to the window and is therefore chiefly in shadow; the model on the left receives full light. As can be seen from the early stages of the painting on Dunstan's canvas, she was, from the painter's point of view, light against a shadowy background. The studio was built in 1936

The Dunstan Demonstration Painting July 1979. This was the painting on which Bernard Dunstan was at work before the students. Reaching this degree of completion within about 6 hours on a canvas of 48 in. × 32 in. – 122 cm × 81 cm represents quite a feat of concentration. The constant light of the north window of Malvern School of Art studio helped to make this possible and perhaps, too, the workmanlike atmosphere engendered in the studio arising in some degree from its good functional design, also contributed. The two models placed against a background of textile printed with big cabbage roses makes a composition in which Dunstan has achieved breadth and unity. A certain amount of detail grasps the attention and the long range of tone from light to shadow, encompasses in this painting, a most delicate and rich treatment of colour

Right: *Roofscape of studios where artists used to congregate*. The need for a north or top light in a studio was so universal in the art world of the past that a roofscape in Fulham or Chelsea in London where artists congregated, would present a vista of complicated dormers, roof lights and sky lights where roofs had been thrust up to catch the essential constant lighting

Glossary

Alla prima painting   Painting—usually from the subject—in one sitting; paint put on in its final colour and tone at the first attempt.

Breadth   Unity of effect. Not, as might be thought, the use of a wide brush, so much as a pulling together of all detail into its right tone relationship to make it subservient to the whole.

Chiaroscuro   The balance of light against shade. Seen when a painter takes a viewpoint that enables him to see the full depth of the shadow as well as the full light. Often this is achieved by the painter's line of sight being at a right angle to the direction of light rays. Typical of seventeenth century painting.

Composition and **compositional work**   A work which is compiled from the artist's knowledge and imagination. It arises from the body of knowledge gleaned through making studies, but relies on visual memory and the creative inner eye. It is the opposite to and complementary to, study. See *Study*.

Cuttlefish bone   The skeletal bone left when the cuttlefish has rotted away; a porous, siliceous mass useful as a mild abrasive.

Cuttlefish sepia ink   A dark fluid emitted as a defensive cloud behind which escape is possible. Collected fresh from this octopus like organism, it makes an excellent, dark brown ink. Dried it can be stored and made into sepia watercolour paint.

Earth colours   Pigments that are made from natural clays stained with iron oxide—hence the rust like tints of Venetian, light and Indian red, the clay like colour of yellow ochre; browns include raw and burnt siena, raw and burnt umber and terre verte, a green. First used by Paleolithic cave painters; permanent.

Glaze   Thin transparent paint layer—see chapter 15.

Grisaille   Monochrome painting in a neutral colour used for underpainting and sometimes for finished work; used thus by Mantegna (National Gallery). See also *Verdaccio*.

Ground   A prepared surface on wood, canvas and paper. There are various preparations suited to egg tempera painting, oil painting, silverpoint etc.

Gypsum   Slaked Plaster of Paris, the main ingredient of Gesso grounds for egg tempera painting.

Impasto   Expressed crudely it is thick paint, but see chapters 13, 14, 15.

Lay in (and also **Build up, Working on** and **Development**)   These are all phrases which attempt to describe the progress of a painting of some complexity, and are fully comprehensible only in conjunction with the actual practice of painting.

Lean painting   Paint without much medium or only that sort of medium which will evaporate away such as distilled turpentine.

Lead   Lead is an ingredient of flake white and Cremnitz white and also driers such as lithage. This is a poisonous chemical but normal precautions such as thorough hand washing means that these materials can be used with reasonable safety.

Lead pencil   The operative core of a pencil is, at the present time, made of graphite. The term 'lead' is retained even though it is a long time since lead was used. Hence 'leads'—the refills for a pair of compasses, propelling pencils, or the slips of graphite sawn up from mineral graphite.

Levigated colour   Finely ground pure pigment. It is ready for grinding in oil to make oil paint or to use with any binder such as yolk of egg in tempera painting. It should be distinguished from *powder colour*, a dry form of poster colour, which already contains a binder.

Monochrome   An initial stage of painting where one colour only is used.

Mahl stick   A bamboo stick about a yard/metre long which has a padded tip (a ball of cotton wool covered with a piece of wash leather tied tightly). Held in the palette hand and resting the padded tip on a dry part of the canvas, the painter can rest his hand and steady it on the shaft. This enables him to paint accurate detail in wet paint without smudging it with the hand. See figure 63 *The Artist in his Studio* by Rembrandt, and *The Studio, Bilting* by John Ward RA.

Medium   Linseed or Poppy oil with which pigment is ground to make oil paint and also a variety of fluids put in the dipper and mixed with oil paint to make it flow. See *Vehicle*.

Oiling out   When repainting on a dry painting, it often helps in the integration of the continued work, to moisten the whole surface. This can be done with a mixture of one part linseed oil to three of turpentine, or with retouching varnish.

Pigment   The colour used to make paint. Minerals, aniline and natural dyestuffs prepared to take the form of levigated colours. See *Levigated*.

Port-crayon   A metal holder in which to fit chalks or conté to make it easier to handle.

Powder colour   To be distinguished from Levigated. See *Levigated*.

Priming   A ground for oil painting. A preparation of which the main ingredients are gesso or chalk, zinc oxide, a little linseed oil and size with which canvas is coated. It is also used on various sorts of board. Proprietary brands of priming, usually acrylic, are available.

Study   A drawing or painting done on the spot from the actual scene or from an object or model; work done from the life model. A study is essentially a means for gathering information, an exercise for developing the visual interpretation of nature or man made objects. Since the development of Impressionism, it has become the accepted and customary way of making a picture. This was not necessarily the case in the Renaissance and almost certainly not for the artists of antiquity such as the Egyptians or Sumerians.

Sanguine   Red chalk, red haematite of iron.

Stump or **tortillion**   Tightly rolled paper or washleather made into a pencil shape and used to blend charcoal, pencil, chalk or pastel. It enables fine detail to be modelled with more control than the broad smear of a finger tip.

Scumble   To draw a brush load of buttery paint lightly over previous painting or canvas, allowing the paint to be caught on the prominences of the surface texture. It allows the previous colour to show through. Unlike a glaze it does not make a covering film, but it is a final surface treatment.

Size   A thin condition of glue. The best is made from parchment shavings or rabbit skin glue.

Underpainting   Preparatory layer of painting. The first layers of a painting in monochrome may deal with drawing only, colour being left to the last stages. See *Grisaille* and *Verdaccio*.

Vehicle   A painting vehicle is a liquid or jelly which is added to the paint to make it more flowing and easier to work with. Sometimes used synonymously with the word *medium* but unlike medium it does not apply to the oil used for making paint. See chapters 13, 14, 15 and under Medium.

Verdaccio   The monochrome used in egg tempera painting—a dun colour made of ivory black, yellow ochre, light red and white.

Zinc oxide   White pigment which makes Chinese white in watercolour, is an ingredient of flake white oil paint or forms a ground for silver point.

Bibliography

D'ANDREA, CENNINO, CENNINI, *Il Libro dell' Arte—Craftsman's Handbook*, translation by Daniel V Thompson Jr, Dover Publications, New York

D'ANDREA, CENNINO, CENNINI, *A Treatise on Painting*, translation by Mrs Merrifield, London, 1844

CHURCH, A H, *The Chemistry of Paints and Painting*, Seeley, London, 1901

DOERNER, MAX, *The Materials of the Artist*, Harrap, London, 1949

EASTLAKE, CHARLES LOCK, *Materials for a History of Oil Painting*, Longman, Brown, Green and Longmans, London, 1847

FAIRHOLT, F W, *A Dictionary of Terms in Art*, c 1870

GLUCK (as she preferred to be addressed, without prefix or initial), *The Dilemma of the Painter and Conservator in the Synthetic Age*, Paper read to the Museums Association Conference, July, 1954

GLUCK, *The Impermanence of Painting in Relation to Artists' Materials*, Royal Society of Arts, April, 1964

HOLMES, SIR CHARLES, *The National Gallery*, 3 volumes, Bell, 1916

LAURIE, A P, *Painter's Methods and Materials*, Dover Publications, New York, 1968; Seeley, London (New Art Library)

MAROGER, JACQUES, *The Secret Formulas and Techniques of the Masters*, Studio, 1948

REDGRAVE, F M, *Redgrave, Richard, CB, RA*, Cassell, 1891

ROTHENSTEIN, SIR JOHN, *Modern English Painters*, Volume I, 1952, Volume II, 1956, Macdonald, London

ROTHENSTEIN, SIR WILLIAM, *Men and Memories*, Volumes I and II, Faber, 1931

ROTHENSTEIN, SIR WILLIAM, *Since Fifty, Men and Memories 1922–1938*, Faber, 1939

SPON, ERNEST, *Workshop Receipts for Manufacturers*, Mechanics and Scientific Amateurs, 1879

Main suppliers of artists' materials

Main Suppliers of Artists' Materials

For all artists' materials

Reeves
PO Box 91
Wealdstone
Harrow HA3 5QN
Middlesex

Reeves Art Shop
178 Kensington High Street
London W8

George Rowney and Co Ltd
10–11 Percy Street
London W1A 2BP

PO Box 10
Bracknell RG12 4ST

Winsor and Newton
Wealdstone
Harrow HA3 5RH
Middlesex

Showroom
51–52 Rathbone Place
London W1P 1AB

USA
555 Winsor Drive
Secancus
New Jersey 07094

Australia
102–104 Reserve Road
Artarmon
New South Wales 2064

C Roberson and Co Ltd
71 Parkway
Regent's Park
London NW1

Also Roberson's medium and Maroger medium

See *Yellow Pages* directory for local art suppliers

Specialist supplier

L Cornelissen and Sons
22 Great Queen Street
Covent Garden
London WC2B 5BH

Artists' colourmen and suppliers of a variety of varnishes, resin media, basic materials, gums, resins, wax and a variety of useful things such as rabbit skin glue and pumice powder

Wengers Limited
Garner Street
Etruria
Stoke-on-Trent ST4 7BQ

For calcined bone

Index

Numerals in *italic* refer to illustrations